Dementia: An Attachme

CW00801490

This interdisciplinary book offers a relational perspective to dementia care drawing on attachment theory and practice. Relevant to professionals and the general public alike, it brings together innovative research and practice in psychotherapy and the creative arts with the lived experience of being a carer. Indeed the book includes insights from professional and personal experience throughout. It also provides exclusive access to Josh Appignanesi's short film, *Ex Memoria*, about his grandmother's experience of dementia, poignantly portrayed by Sara Kestelman. Chapters include the experience of caring for a sister with dementia; the importance of an attachment perspective in theory and practice; a new approach to understanding the possible origins of dementia in trauma; contemporary understandings from clinical and research arenas; the description of a leading-edge project providing psychotherapeutic work; and an innovative creative arts and reminiscence European-wide family intervention for those living with dementia.

Written in accessible language, *Dementia: An Attachment Approach* will be of great interest to people living with dementia, as well as those working with, and caring for, people with dementia in a variety of contexts including nurses, doctors and psychiatrists, clinical and counselling psychologists, social workers, health and social care workers, family carers and psychotherapists, as well as creative arts practitioners and policymakers.

Kate White is a training therapist, supervisor, researcher and teacher at The Bowlby Centre, UK. She is series editor of *The Bowlby Centre Monograph Series* and was formerly editor of the journal *Attachment: New Directions in Psychotherapy and Relational Psychoanalysis*. Kate was previously a senior lecturer in district nursing at London South Bank University, UK. She has edited and co-edited many books on a variety of issues in relation to psychoanalysis, including attachment, culture, sexuality, trauma and the body.

Angela Cotter is a Jungian analyst, training supervisor and teacher. She is Head of Research at the Minster Centre and a Visiting Lecturer at Regent's University London, UK. She is a former NHS nursing home manager and action researcher, working with older people and people with dementia. Since her doctorate in 1990, her research has focused on the phenomenon of the wounded healer, which informs her work on the significance of the current growth of dementia and ways of supporting those who care for people with dementia.

Hazel Leventhal trained as a psychotherapist at The Bowlby Centre, where she chaired the Clinical Forum for several years. Her previous works include the play *My Sister, Disappearing* and a book entitled *Soul Stories*. She has worked as a Samaritan and is a member of The Alzheimer's Society and has done some publicity work on their behalf. She has a private practice in Aspley Heath, UK.

The Bowlby Centre Monograph Series

A series of books taken from the annual John Bowlby Memorial Conference and other conferences, produced in association with The Bowlby Centre, London.

Titles in the series:

Dementia: An Attachment Approach
Edited by Kate White, Angela Cotter and Hazel Leventhal

Addictions From an Attachment Perspective: Do Broken Bonds and Early Trauma Lead to Addictive Behaviours?
Edited by Richard Gill

From Broken Attachments to Earned Security: The Role of Empathy in Therapeutic Change
Edited by Andrew Odgers

Talking Bodies: How do we Integrate Working with the Body in Psychotherapy from an Attachment and Relational Perspective?
Edited by Kate White

Terror Within and Without: Attachment and Disintegration: Clinical Work on the Edge
Edited by Judy Yellin and Orit Badouk Epstein

Shattered States: Disorganised Attachment and its Repair
Edited by Kate White

Trauma and Attachment
Edited by Sarah Benamer and Kate White

Unmasking Race, Culture, and Attachment in the Psychoanalytic Space
Edited by Kate White

Sexuality and Attachment in Clinical Practice
Edited by Kate White and Joseph Schwartz

Touch: Attachment and the Body
Edited by Kate White

For further information about this series please visit
https://www.routledge.com/The-Bowlby-Centre-
Monograph-Series/book-series/KARNJBMCM

Dementia: An Attachment Approach

Edited by Kate White,
Angela Cotter and Hazel Leventhal

Routledge
Taylor & Francis Group

LONDON AND NEW YORK

First published 2019
by Routledge
2 Park Square, Milton Park, Abingdon, Oxon OX14 4RN

and by Routledge
711 Third Avenue, New York, NY 10017

Routledge is an imprint of the Taylor & Francis Group, an informa business

© 2019 editorial matter and individual chapters, Kate White, Angela Cotter and Hazel Leventhal; other individual chapters, the contributors

The right of Kate White, Angela Cotter and Hazel Leventhal to be identified as the authors of the editorial material, and of the authors for their individual chapters, has been asserted in accordance with sections 77 and 78 of the Copyright, Designs and Patents Act 1988.

British Library Cataloging-in-Publication Data
A catalogue record for this book is available from the British Library

Library of Congress Cataloging-in-Publication Data
Names: White, Kate, 1949- editor.
Title: Dementia : an attachment approach / edited by Kate White, Angela Cotter and Hazel Leventhal.
Description: Milton Park, Abingdon, Oxon ; New York, NY : Routledge, 2018. | Includes bibliographical references.
Identifiers: LCCN 2018020865 (print) | LCCN 2018021957 (ebook) | ISBN 9780429449499 (Master eBook) | ISBN 9781138327030 (hbk) | ISBN 9781138327054 (pbk) | ISBN 9780429449499 (ebk)
Subjects: LCSH: Dementia. | Attachment behavior.
Classification: LCC RC521 (ebook) | LCC RC521 .D4528 2018 (print) | DDC 616.8/31—dc23
LC record available at https://lccn.loc.gov/2018020865

ISBN: 978-1-138-32703-0 (hbk)
ISBN: 978-1-138-32705-4 (pbk)
ISBN: 978-0-429-44949-9 (ebk)

Typeset in Times
by Apex CoVantage, LLC

Contents

Contributors

Josh Appignanesi is a writer/director based in London. He recently co-directed *The New Man,* the acclaimed feature documentary, with Devorah Baum. He is now writing and directing art world psycho-thriller *Female Human Animal.* He previously directed the award-winning comedy feature *The Infidel,* starring Omid Djalili, Richard Schiff, Matt Lucas, Miranda Hart and Archie Panjabi, scripted by David Baddiel. His debut feature film *Song of Songs,* starring Natalie Press, won awards at Edinburgh and London Film Festivals and was critically acclaimed. He also co-wrote the Sarah Jessica Parker-starring rom-com *All Roads lead to Rome* and makes shorts, commercials and artist's film, working with talent from John Malkovich, David Tennant, Tom Hiddleston, Sara Kestelman and Michelle Dockery, and collaborating with artist Martin Creed among others.
He mentors, advises and teaches internationally for various institutions including the London Film School, the Met Film School, Guardian Masterclasses and Film London.

Richard Bowlby, Patron of The Bowlby Centre, worked as a scientific photographer in various medical research institutions where he produced visual aids for communicating research findings. He now gives lectures to health care professionals using video material and personal insights to promote a much broader understanding of his father's work on attachment theory. He supports a range of organisations that address challenging attachment issues, and is seeking ways to help the general public benefit from a better understanding of attachment relationships.

Angela Cotter is a Jungian analyst, training supervisor and teacher, Head of Research at the Minster Centre and a Visiting Lecturer at Regent's University, London. For many years, she taught the last part of the lifecycle at the Bowlby Centre emphasising the central role of attachment in dementia care. She first became interested in dementia when her step-grandmother developed Alzheimer's disease in 1965. This informed her later work as a nurse, as a NHS nursing home manager and action researcher working to improve older people's, and their carers', experience. This led into involvement in policy-making and in the "new culture of dementia care" combining her psychotherapeutic perspective in her clinical work and research. Her work has included a co-operative action research study about the use of creative arts within the NHS involving people with dementia and their staff. Since her doctorate in 1990 on this subject, she has researched and explored the phenomenon of the wounded healer, and this informs her work on the significance of the current growth of dementia for individuals and within the collective.

Susie M. D. Henley is a Clinical Psychologist specialising in working with people with long-term conditions such as dementia. Following a degree in psychology and a PhD in neuroscience, Susie trained as a clinical psychologist and subsequently spent five years as clinical lead for the psychological intervention service at the Specialist Cognitive Disorders Service at the National Hospital for Neurology and Neurosurgery in London. Susie developed the psychological input to this neurology-led dementia diagnosis and treatment service and offered a short-term therapeutic intervention to both patients and their families. The service specialises in supporting those with rare, inherited and early-onset dementias. Susie's work ranged from explaining brain-behaviour links to patients, to helping families develop their understanding of symptoms and supporting people through the many challenges that a dementia diagnosis presents. Her research focused on developing early tests for memory problems in Alzheimer's disease, as well as more qualitative evaluation of the lived experience of people with dementia and their families, and how their needs could be better met.

Sara Kestelman: an Olivier Award winner as Fraulein Schneider in Sam Mendes' *Cabaret* at The Donmar, Sara has appeared extensively with the Royal Shakespeare Company, Royal National Theatre, on screen, radio and in the West End. She created the role of Margrethe Bohr in Michael Frayn's award winning play *Copenhagen*, and has appeared in many musicals including *Fiddler on the Roof, Nine* and was Coco Chanel in *Coco*. Recently Sara was in the BAFTA winning series two *In the Flesh* and in *Maigret*. She is a published poet and songwriter and has performed her one-woman show *All About Me!* internationally. A reader with the charity *InterAct Reading Service* which is dedicated to recoverers from stroke, she has made a documentary film, *Yes, But That's Not All!* with Amanda Brennan and BASK Films about her work with one remarkable woman, Nan Millard. As part of the centenary of WW1, she directed a new musical *Brass* for the National Youth Music Theatre winning Best Musical Production. Her most recent films were *The Last Sparks At Sundown* winner of Best Comedy in the Chicago Comedy Festival, and several award winning short films: *The Last Dance, Pardon The Intrusion* and *Prick Thy Neighbour.* She played the lead, a woman with dementia, in Josh Appignanesi's award winning *Ex Memoria.* Most recent theatre was Tony Kushner's *iHo* at The Hampstead Theatre followed by a critically acclaimed performance in a new play *Filthy Business* also at Hampstead. In the 2017 Bath summer festival she did *The Lady In The Van.* When the Royal Mail celebrated the

RSC's 50th anniversary, her image as Titania in Peter Brook's RSC production of *A Midsummer Night's Dream* was used on the £1.00 stamp, and next year the theatre and performance department of the V&A are creating an archive of her professional work spanning 52 years.

Sally Knocker: almost Sally's entire working life of over 30 years has been at a national level influencing dementia care development with a particular focus on the importance of activity and occupation. Having trained in drama-therapy, Sally is passionate about valuing people's personal stories and bringing variety, movement and fun to daily life. She is a Consultant Trainer with Dementia Care Matters supporting the creation of Butterfly Households® across the United Kingdom, Ireland, Canada, Australia and the USA. Sally is the author of *Loving, the Essence of Being a Butterfly in Dementia Care* the seventh in the Dementia Care Matters *Feelings Matter Most* series. Sally also has a part-time role with the charity Opening Doors, London facilitating a Rainbow Memory Café support group for lesbian, gay, bisexual and trans (LGBT) people living with a dementia and their partners and friends. She is also a volunteer with the European Reminiscence Network running *Remembering Yesterday, Caring Today* arts-based reminiscence groups in the community.

Hazel Leventhal trained as a psychotherapist at The Bowlby Centre where she taught the mid-life part of The Life Cycle seminar and chaired the Clinical Forum for three years. She was a carer for her father and her elder sister, who suffered from early-onset Alzheimer's disease, and has written about these experiences in a play called *My Sister, Disappearing*. She has also recently finished writing a book called *Soul Stories*. She has worked as a Samaritan and is a member of The Alzheimer's Society and has done some publicity work on their behalf. She has a private practice in Aspley Heath.

Anastasia Patrikiou: after qualifying and working as an architect Anastasia trained as a Person-Centred Counsellor at Strathclyde University and subsequently as an Attachment-based Psychoanalytic Psychotherapist at The Bowlby Centre. She has extensive clinical experience arising from a broad range of settings which includes the NHS, the voluntary sector, the private hospital sector in inpatient, day and outpatient care and her private practice. She set up and managed a pioneering, pilot "Talking Therapies" programme for Age UK Camden, funded by the Department of Health, which offered therapy to older people with dementia and to older people from black and minority ethnic groups. This was subsequently mainstreamed. In recent years she has worked extensively with people with eating disorders both privately and in hospital settings and is interested in how early attachment and relational trauma may impact our ability to nourish and be nourished.

Jane Sherwood trained at the University of Birmingham and the University of Nottingham, to become a social worker. She worked with clients of all ages in the community, before transferring to hospital settings mainly to develop services for families with children who were ill or who had disabilities. Throughout her professional career she found attachment theory provided an invaluable framework for making sense of the challenges in people's lives. She later served as a Disability Appeal Tribunal member, but in 2010 identified a pressing need for someone to start examining the life histories of people who have developed dementia, an area of little apparent interest to formal research teams despite the urgency of the search for clues about the origins of this distressing condition. In order to make time to attend to this herself she had to give up her other work, but was rewarded when she found that her results offered support for John Bowlby's observation that "from a new perspective, a familiar landscape can sometimes appear very different". Sir Richard Bowlby has since presented the findings of this pilot dementia study in various academic settings, most notably at the UCLA conference on *Affect Regulation and Healing of the Self* in March 2014.

Pam Schweitzer was founder and Artistic Director of Age Exchange Theatre Trust from 1983–2005, the first full-time professional theatre company to specialise in touring reminiscence theatre across the UK and Europe. In 2000 she was awarded the MBE for services to Reminiscence and she continues to direct the European Reminiscence Network, lecturing, directing and training in reminiscence. She is an Honorary Fellow of the University of Greenwich. Reminiscence is a vital way to stimulate communication and promote confidence and self-worth in people with dementia. Her approach is to give those who care for people with dementia a clear sense of how reminiscence can be used to greatly improve their quality of life, opening the world's first Reminiscence Centre in London in 1987, as a focus for professional training, a meeting place for people of all generations and cultures to participate in reminiscence projects. She has published widely on her work – see www.pamschweitzer.com

Valerie Sinason is a poet, writer, child, adolescent and adult psychotherapist and adult psychoanalyst. She was Founder Director of the Clinic for Dissociative Studies until her retirement and remains a Consultant. She is former President of the Institute for Psychotherapy and Disability (IPD) and Honorary Consultant Psychotherapist at the University of Cape Town Child Guidance Clinic; Patron of the Dorchester Trust; Chair of Trustees of the First People Art Centre – Nieu Bethesda Arts Foundation.
Her extensive writing includes more than 120 papers and chapters. Furthermore, she has written, edited and co-edited more than fourteen books. These include a revised edition of her seminal book *Mental Handicap and the Human Condition* (2010), a second edition of her edited book *Attachment, Trauma and Multiplicity: Working with Dissociative Identity Disorder* (2010) and *Trauma Attachment and Dissociation* (2012). Her most recent co-edited books are *Shattered But Unbroken: Voices of Triumph and Testimony* with Amelia van der Merwe (2016), and *Holistic Therapy for People with Dissociative Identity Disorder* (2017) with Pat Frankish.

Kate White is a training therapist, supervisor and teacher at The Bowlby Centre. She was until recently editor of the journal, *Attachment: New Directions in Psychotherapy and Relational Psychoanalysis*. She currently continues in her role as Series Editor, *The John Bowlby Centre Conference Monographs*, now into its tenth volume. Prior to training as a psychotherapist Kate was a senior lecturer at The South Bank University, London, where she developed an innovative diploma in district nursing. This is where her interest in the care of those who become vulnerable through dementia, memory loss and ageing originated. The perspective provided by attachment theory has, in her view, a great deal to offer carers and family members alike. In addition to working as an individual psychotherapist, Kate writes about psychotherapy education and runs workshops on the themes of attachment and trauma in clinical practice and dementia care.

She has edited three books: *Unmasking Race, Culture and Attachment in the Psychoanalytic Space: What do we see? What do we think? What do we feel?* (2006); *Touch: Attachment and the Body* (2004); and *Talking Bodies: How do we Integrate Working with the Body in Psychotherapy from an Attachment and Relational Perspective?* (2013) and co-edited three others: *Sexuality and Attachment in Clinical Practice* (2007), a second with Sarah Benamer *Trauma and Attachment* (2008) and a third with Judy Yellin, *Shattered States, Disorganised Attachment and its Repair,* (2012).

She is currently co-editing a book with Robbie Duschinsky, *Trauma and Loss: Key Texts from the John Bowlby Archive*.

Acknowledgements

Thank you to those involved in organising the conference out of which has emerged this exciting book. The creativity of that event and the excellence of its contributors can now reach a much wider audience.

A special thank you to staff at both Karnac and Routledge for their support and patience during the editing process.

Thank you also to Mark Linington for his ongoing encouragement and belief in the unique vision of this book.

Kate White, Angela Cotter and Hazel Leventhal
July 2018

Foreword

This is an exciting book which is much needed and timely, because it places emotions and psychological needs at the centre stage of what must surely be the future of dementia care provision, not just in the UK but internationally. Importantly it also begins to break down the false divisions between people living with dementia, their family and friends and professional caregivers. It makes clear that these emotions and psychological needs are profoundly the same for *us all*, (Knocker, 2015).

I will illustrate the implications of this from my insights into the work we do at Dementia Care Matters, an organisation that aims to support people to continue to live well with dementia through culture change programmes. A quote from a senior care worker at the first Butterfly Home created in 1995 (Note 1) is significant: "I've been everyone to them. I've been a husband, a brother and a father. I've had to be that person for them. I find it easy. It's keeping them human, keeping them feeling human." (Sheard, 2008, p. 33).

The person had no previous experience in care work before being employed there. Dr David Sheard, the founder of Dementia Care Matters, and Anne Fretwell, the manager of the home, were clear that they were not looking for *staff* with years of care experience, qualifications or traditional training in dementia awareness. They were looking for *people* who came from a place of heart. They realised everyone needed the emotional competence to *be* alongside someone with compassion and without judgment, just the same as we all need when we find ourselves in a difficult emotional place. The quote reveals an implicit understanding that the actual identity staff represent to people could be transient. However, the important thing they were expected to convey, in embodying significant roles in the past lives of people with dementia, was a feeling of security and unconditional love specifically needed in that moment, a theme extensively explored in this new book.

As Sheard explains, training needs to focus first "on staff feelings and exploring the concept of self and of their own 'being'. . . .. If we are to enable staff to connect to others they have to feel able to connect to themselves", (Sheard, 2007, p. 39).

Using this attachment approach, the most important training workshop for nursing and care staff is when we invite people to bring in three personal objects which convey something about who they are and their own emotional story in life. During this powerful sharing, we experience significant feelings, learning about the pivotal people, memories and events in people's lives that have shaped who they are. We learn the things that bring people comfort, joy and security, and also some of the very painful losses and past traumas that we carry with us. The importance of this style of learning is how our own emotional lives have parallels in enabling us to connect more intuitively in supporting people living with dementia.

As Kate White shares in her chapter, when we start to nurture emotionally self-aware caregivers, the positive possibilities are inspiring. She highlights how revisiting "the different stages in our life stories and attachment histories can lead to deepening intimacy and the renewal of emotional bonds with the creation of new meanings". This is not to underestimate the huge impact of the losses associated with living with dementia. These specific losses for the person themselves and those who are close to them are movingly described in Hazel Leventhal's account of supporting her sister.

By focusing on dementia as an emotional experience, where the full range of human emotions remain, this book aims to challenge the prevalent paradigm in society and in the media of seeing dementia as only a "tragedy", something to be "suffered" and where "little can be done" to make a difference.

However, people living with dementia do find themselves in fearful and unfamiliar situations and searching for reassurances that they are not alone or abandoned. The book provides extraordinary insights into understanding that many expressions of "behaviour" in living with dementia are linked to insecure attachments, something also explored in detail by Tanner (2017) in his book on *Embracing Touch in Dementia Care*. As Kate White says, it is evident that "attachment is linked to the human response to fear and is most clearly evident where there are threats of separation and abandonment." She further explains: "in the case of secure attachment we have come to understand ourselves as lovable and capable of loving others because we have been exposed to repeated and sufficient responsiveness and attuned soothing for us to internalise this feeling".

This book asserts that people living with dementia search inside themselves for a sense of safety but this is often now eroded and so needs to be provided by those who support them.

Providing this is *the* core quality and skill we are looking for in a professional caregiver. As Sheard describes in his concept of the "attached professional" the need in health and social care is for people who are entirely comfortable with "being loving" at work because it is at the core of who they are.

The focus of some safeguarding policies which emphasise the "dangers of emotional involvement" have neglected to acknowledge that the biggest safeguarding concern of all is where people do not feel loved, valued and understood (Sheard, 2015). This lack of emotional safeguarding lies in outdated concepts of the need for "detached" workers and a lack of understanding that emotional safety and wellbeing is where our vigilant attention should always remain. For far too long the rhetoric engrained in the majority of "old culture" care was that it was not "professional" to hug, kiss or cry with someone and it was not appropriate to share anything personal about ourselves in the workplace. It is heartening in our culture change work how many leaders, nurses, care workers and housekeepers describe how relieved they are to be given permission to show love and friendship to people. They describe working in a place of attachment as having a sense of "coming home" and relief at finally working somewhere where what they have always believed was the right way to "be" with people is supported.

In Butterfly Households, we also focus on creating environments that enable a sense of freedom and belonging as well as invitations to feel busy and purposeful. The items that fill hallways, lounges and dining rooms are not just "clutter" but can also be understood as attachment objects, connected with people's past work, home lives or offer opportunities to nurture others such as dolls and soft toys. For some they are a life line to being restored to their sense of core identity and worth. When emotional competency, an understanding of attachment theory and the importance of emotions attached to objects are fully adopted as a model of care and support this is when the magic of "being attached" really starts to happen.

This links with fascinating insights into the language of dementia as being symbolic and how we need to become interpreters in this new language. Anastasia Patrikiou's case studies of people living with dementia receiving counselling give rich examples of these. For instance a woman's preoccupation with an unstable chair as a powerful way of describing the "precariousness of her core self" and another woman's concern about the poor condition of a plant in the therapy room as a way of her communicating much of what was taking place inside her. As Angela Cotter says, very often people living with dementia *are* communicating important things to us, but the fault often lies in us in not listening well enough to the different ways in which these feelings are being conveyed. She also echoes what I have experienced myself, that many people living with dementia "cut right through to the essence of relationship with no holds barred". I remember a time when I was feeling vulnerable and sad in my own life, a woman living in a care home in Wales who had been a lay preacher took my hands in hers and said kindly and quietly, "I feel you might need a prayer with me." I felt truly cherished in that moment.

Jane Sherwood's chapter challenges us further to explore the extent to which our early life experiences in relation to loss of parental or attachment figures might actually be a causal factor in dementia. If we turn this round, the relevance of an emotional "secure base" in early life might well have a protective element, if not in terms of preventing the onset of dementia, certainly in terms of the extent to which we have a resilience to adapting to its impact on our lives.

This is not just a book for academics or therapists with an interest in people living with dementia, it is for *all* those at the vanguard of promoting the "feelings matter most" approach as integral to the very best dementia care in the future. It provides a message of hope as well as an urgent call to action to all service providers. The challenge is to ensure this philosophy is at the heart of all care organisations transforming how they recruit, support and educate future leaders and care teams in creating a genuinely attached and loving group of people at work.

Sally Knocker

Note

1   www.dementiacarematters.com

References

Knocker, S. (2015). *Loving – the Essence of Being a Butterfly in Dementia Care*. London: Hawker Publications.

Sheard, D. (2007). *Being – An Approach to Life and Dementia*. London: Dementia Care Matters.

Sheard, D. (2008). *Inspiring Leadership Matters in Dementia Care*. London: Dementia Care Matters.

Sheard, D. (2015). Safeguarding emotions really matters in dementia care. *Journal of Dementia Care, 23,* (4) 22–25.

Tanner, L. (2017). *Embracing Touch in Dementia Care*. London: Jessica Kingsley.

Chapter 1

Introduction

Setting the scene

Angela Cotter

Following the success of our conference I am delighted to be giving you an overview of the conference papers and the additional material we have decided to include. This monograph brings together much of my previous experience both personal and professional and this chapter includes some reflections on this. The book's interdisciplinary focus is enriching and enlightening. However, before introducing the chapters, I want to highlight an overall issue that I feel deserves putting on the agenda from the start.

As I wrote at the time of the Conference:

> It is the day before the conference and I am full of my usual trepidation and confusion when I am due to give a paper about memory loss and/or dementia. I do a last-minute search for my books, and for literature and other resources to support me and cannot find them. Then I find them in the place where they should have been first of all. This is not uncommon especially as I have grown older and have more resources to file and search for. However, what is unusual is my anxiety and fear that I shall have lost everything and so will not be able to give the paper – that although I have been working on this introduction over the weeks I shall find I have nothing to draw on today. The prospect of today fills me with dread because I seem to have said everything before, and had better words before too. Then in a search for distraction I look at a piece of creative writing I wrote about my being a fool in the land of the wise and cannot understand a contrived riddle in it. Who wrote this? Was it me?

What is going on? Back in the early 1990s I was involved in a British Psychological Society conference about psychotherapy and dementia. It was probably one of the first. Valerie Sinason gave a keynote paper in which she spoke about her own counter-transference to the subject – her own reactions – being enacted in her fearing she had lost the details of where the conference was going to be held in Birmingham and on top of that had lost contact details for the group of organisers. Our own reactions to the subject often mirror the possible experience of the person with dementia. And this is not surprising - dementia is very frightening, apparently confronting us with the prospect of "losing our brain" (Sinason,

1992), "our mind" (Sutton, 1994) or "the loss of what makes us uniquely human" (Kaplan, 1990). This makes us anxious. According to an Alzheimer's Research Trust YouGov poll conducted in 2015 (which you will find if you do a search on the Alzheimer's Society website) 52 percent of people over 60 cite Alzheimer's Disease as one of their top three concerns about being in the later years of life. An Alzheimer's Society survey in 2008 also showed that half of all UK adults believe that dementia remains a condition plagued by stigma.

We chose to give the conference the title "Attachment, Memory Loss and Ageing" because memory loss is sometimes, and sometimes not, an antecedent to dementia and something that touches many of us in our experience of ageing. It is a way in to talking about dementia. I rather suspect that memory loss touches many of us whatever age we are but we may become more sensitised to it – more aware of it – as we age. In an over-cognitive society, the fear of losing our cognitive capacities, of not knowing, of maybe therefore being seen as foolish and shamed because of this can be terrifying. There is the accompanying fear of being seen as "useless", and no longer being sure who I am because what defines me – what constitutes my identity in this society – is often rather more concerned with what I do than who I am – what I produce rather than how human I am as a being or how "being" I am as a human. Arguably, our society also values independence rather than interdependence; chases after perfection and is intolerant of imperfection. Yet the reality is that we all live in a very dependent society – for example, how long would many of us last if the supermarket supplies were cut off for an extended time? And increasingly we hear that it is recognition of our imperfections that leads to change and transformation. A central strand of Jung's (1951/1966, p. 116) "wounded healer" concept is that the healer has to recognise their own quintessential woundedness (i.e. the woundedness that belongs to all of us by virtue of being human) to allow the patient (i.e. the one in the place of being wounded) to be able to contact their own healer within. If the healer cannot do this, the relationship has no place to go and becomes one of power over rather than empowerment. Or as Brene Brown (2010a, 2010b) puts it, she of the TED talk that has received over five million hits, recognition of their vulnerability is a key characteristic of those who lead whole-hearted lives.

That is the good news. However, in this society, it can be very hard for us to recognise our vulnerability. I suggest that we still want to be perfect (and much of our standard setting culture implies that we can be) and we often have fiercely critical inner voices that shame us when we do not measure up. In this context, the opportunity for projection onto people with memory loss and dementia is rife. When I first worked in the NHS as a nurse, it was not uncommon to hear stereotyping of people with dementia as not "sensible", because the staff could not follow the words they said. They were also seen as not understanding anything because of their confusion and consigned often to a world of being talked over and about rather than to. There has been much work to address these issues since then and some incredibly heart-warming and innovative work, as we can see in this monograph, but it would not be surprising if some of those attitudes still lurk in staff in poorly paid situations, with little training and no framework for under-standing dementia. Isabel Menzies-Lyth's (1959) paper about the functioning of social systems as a defence against anxiety still holds true. The depersonalisation of patients and task orientation of the staff defends them against the traumatic situations they encounter in their work, where being open day after day can be too painful without support and encouragement. And these attitudes may not only be in staff but also in individuals in society too.

What is the alternative? Firstly, there is a need for a greater awareness of the issues, and this book, based on the conference papers, is intended to address that. We made the decision to revise the title to *Dementia: An Attachment Approach* to be clearer and more direct. Secondly, we need to dispel some of the myths in rela-tion to people with dementia in particular. In my work with people with advanced dementia of different kinds I have found that the fault in not understanding – in seeing them as not sensible – lies rather more often in me than in them. I will give some examples. There is a tendency for people with dementia to talk metaphorically rather than factually. Therefore in many of the interviews I have conducted with people with dementia, the range of my understanding is defined by my ability to understand their metaphors or allusions. I recall visiting a participant in a research project for the second time in a care home. I had previously visited in the spring and this was summer a couple of months later. It was difficult to know how to begin the interview. I explained about the project again – that it was about moving from hospital to a care home – and that I wanted to talk with her about what life was like for her now. I said that I had been before in April, to which she said, "April is the cruellest month". I recognised this as the first line from T. S. Eliot's "Wasteland" – a poem about memory indeed, recognised as perhaps the greatest modernist poem – but to my mind quite impenetrable. I feel like a bear of little brain when I read it and wish I had a Christopher Robin to hand to help. But I knew the first stanza:

April is the cruellest month, breeding
Lilacs out of the dead land, mixing
Memory and desire, stirring
Dull roots with spring rain.

(Eliot, 1922/1963, p. 63)

What was being said here? On one level, she might just have been free-associating to my mentioning April. But if this were someone in my therapy prac-tice I would assume there was meaning behind the free association. At the time and since, I felt that she was both recognising that we had met in April – and by met I mean connected – and also chiding me for perhaps having woken something up in her that I had not followed through by visiting more regularly and nurturing the symbolic lilacs. Or perhaps she picked up on the fact that I was feeling guilty that as a researcher I did not have a regular and ongoing relationship with her. There are many other possible meanings as well. However, what she said was not senseless but a very economical communication that just might have been very profound. Yet it all hinges on the knowledge of the literary reference.

I have often found that some people with dementia cut right through to the essence of relationship with no holds barred. There can be a truth telling aspect to it that is both challenging and refreshing. It is somewhat akin to the place of the fool in theatre – such as seen in some of Shakespeare's plays – the fool who is no fool at all – who can speak the truth cutting across all the social conventions and expectations. I have a second story from when I was a NHS nursing home manager to illustrate this point. You have to understand here that I was the most senior person in the home to get the full force of this story. There was a resident with Creutzfeldt-Jakob disease who lived in the home who I will call Nora. It was November 5th. The home as a newly designed unit had a built in conservatory. The staff had set up a firework display and we went down to watch it. I became caught up in the show and the child in me woke up as I said, entranced, "Oh, look at that one, Nora, that's a pretty one. That's really lovely." She looked back at me and said very gently but firmly "And what a silly ass you are!" And then we both fell about laughing in our shared and divine foolishness.

So we need to claim – to own – our own inherent foolishness and vulnerability to hear the voices of people with dementia, and to allow ourselves to be open to expanding our awareness about the subject. Perhaps this is about also connecting with the soul within – the part of the soul that remains intact and profoundly human throughout life. And I suggest we need to be gentle with ourselves about that always and especially as we read these chapters.

At the start of the conference we screened the very moving short film "Ex Memoria" which conveys the experience of someone with dementia in a care home. It really communicates this from the perspective of the person with dementia in the way that it is filmed. The maker of the film, Josh Appignanesi, was not able to come to the conference but Sara Kestelman, who takes the central role, joined us in discussion after the film. She shared with us a poem about her mother, which can be found following Josh's chapter where he outlines his reflections as the director of the film. This film, funded by the Wellcome Trust, was made for educational purposes and can be downloaded and viewed on the internet at https://vimeo.com/133611676, password: Wellcome. There is I feel much that can be learnt from it about how we can be empathic to the situation of individuals with dementia. We suggest you view this film first, as we did at the beginning of the conference, because we want to place the experience of those living with dementia centre stage.

Sara's poem is followed by Kate White's chapter where she writes about "An attachment approach to understanding and living well with dementia". There is an ever-increasing awareness of the importance of relationship with people with dementia – of a relational perspective – as I hope that I have begun to convey. This has often been presented under the person-centred rubric in terms of counselling and therapy. This is important, but an attachment perspective also has a lot to offer and Kate's chapter is the first that emphasises its importance, bringing together work on attachment and dementia interwoven with her own experience. It is a heartfelt chapter echoing her vision wrought in experience, a vision that is behind the conference and this book. I have found the slides she presents very useful too, they sum up a great deal in a way that is accessible, as I found out when she presented two at a session for a carers' group that we facilitated recently. One of the aspects that I feel is tragic here is that those around people with dementia often do not have a framework with which to understand some behaviours that might be described as attachment-seeking such as when someone repeatedly calls out for his or her mother. Further, often when people have very advanced dementia they prefer not to use words at all whether or not they have any impairment of their verbal capacity. For example, a resident in a nursing home, whom I interviewed, spent most of her time staring wordlessly at a carriage clock given to her by her brother, at that time the key or primary attachment figure in her life. This clock accompanied her wherever she went in her institutional chair because the staff had been sensitive enough to let it sit on the attached table. Her silence was hard for me to bear because it was so eloquently painful on a symbolic level but when I did allow myself to relax into it she turned to me with a shy smile that seemed to say it all. It was like she recognised that I had got it. In the jargon, as I understand it, this clock was a transitional object that connected her with her brother and gave her a sense of a secure base – of an internal safe place. Had I not known about the importance of the clock from the staff I would have perhaps understood this differently as being about her watching the clock – in the sense of watching time pass. I might have therefore understood it negatively.

Then we have Susie Henley's presentation about the contemporary understanding of the aetiology, diagnosis and treatment approaches in relation to dementia, as well as including the support available for people with dementia and where it can be found. The conference organising team included this because we felt that it was very important for us to understand the context and current understanding of memory loss and dementia. Susie makes the point that lack of awareness among the public and professionals, alongside limited resources, remain a barrier to good practice. Her chapter addresses this by providing clear and useful information. This is an essential part of increasing our awareness of the subject.

Following this, Sir Richard Bowlby's chapter discusses the proposal that the precursors to dementia lie in early trauma. He cites the findings of Jane Sherwood's pilot research study, which show that the development of dementia in old age appears to be linked to cumulative early loss in the maternal ancestral line. Then he elucidates this thesis by presenting research relevant to the development of dementia in some people and not in others from an attachment and neuroscience perspective, illustrating with examples from his own family tree. This exploration of trauma and the transgenerational transmission of trauma as an antecedent to the development of dementia is a very exciting development in the field which is further explored in the following chapter by Jane Sherwood whose genealogical research is cited by Sir Richard. She presents a strong argument in this chapter to support her conclusion that "the origins of dementia, and ways of intercepting it, may be proving elusive because we have yet to contemplate the possibility that psychology could hold the key that will unlock the complex biological puzzle". Serious contemplation of this possibility, floated by Tom Kitwood (1997) earlier, is long overdue and it is very heartening to read her justification of the need for it.

It is important here to remember that discussions of dementia have been framed historically very much in terms of it being solely an organic disease, i.e. associated brain changes which can be physically seen and diagnosed. While this is in part true, we are indebted here to the work of Tom Kitwood – a very significant figure in what became known as "the new culture of dementia care" in the 1990s – for his challenge to this concept as a polymath including his being a scientist. His argument was that any diagnosis remains equivocal. As he said in 1997: "All the common forms of neuropathology that are associated with the main dementias are also found in the brains of people who have no cognitive impairment" (Kitwood, 1997, p. 24).

This includes some form of cerebral atrophy. So in his view there is no way that the dementias are an organic disease pure and simple. There are some other factors operating. There is also no consistent correlation between degree of dementia assessed in the living person and the extent of neuropathology found post-mortem. The greatest difficulties, however, arise with those people who have been diagnosed with dementia on clinical or neuropsychological criteria but whose brains on post-mortem do not show any signs of dementia beyond what is normal for their age. He cites the highest reported figure in this category in 1997 as being 34 percent. My feeling about this is that it opens the door to looking at psychogenic causes such as trauma. Of course, these may result in brain changes and therefore fit into the organic disease model. The situation is complicated. Kitwood however also spoke to this when he posited that a form of "rementia" might occur – a repairing of the brain – if people are treated in a way that maximises their personhood. His view was that the malignant social psychology whereby someone with confusion is treated as confused then becomes more confused and so on, needed to be redressed with a focus on really listening to and hearing what the person with dementia was saying – seeing beyond the disease to the person. This, for example, echoes the debates that happened much earlier in relation to schizophrenia. The very fact that antecedents in relation to early trauma are now being considered in both conditions is a great step forward.

Pam Schweitzer's chapter about the innovative European-wide project *Remembering Yesterday and Caring Today,* which she founded twenty years ago, explores one of the important aspects of how we make meaning of our lives is in the construction of our narratives about them. Reminiscence works with this capacity – and allows people to tell their story. Importantly it also concentrates on what people can remember rather than what they cannot. On a common sense view, if I am anxious because I am losing my memory particularly about recent events, working with what I can remember is likely to bolster my self-esteem and redress the balance. When I was involved in an action research project about the use of creative arts with people with advanced dementia and the staff who work with them, it was very interesting to discover that participation of both staff and people with dementia in different forms of creative arts was an equalising process (Cotter et al., 2001). The staff had to recognise that sometimes the skills of the people with dementia were greater than theirs. They were shocked to see that people with dementia were better than they were at some things. This is not always obvious in a care home or (as then) a ward setting. So, for example, a resident who had been a dressmaker and specialised in beautiful delicate embroidery was able to contribute exquisite work to a collage about the seaside. Another brought their artistic skills to bear in their drawing of their hand. It is a mistake to think that memory loss applies equally in every area of life. Reminiscence brings into focus what can be remembered.

Hazel Leventhal's contribution addresses the experience of carers from her own unique story of her relationship with her sister who developed Alzheimer's in her fifties. Hazel, like Kate and Anastasia, is an attachment-based psychotherapist and her reflections, with a focus embedded in her perspective, are most moving. I recall a key piece of research by Melanie Henwood, published in 1998, about carers and their experience of the NHS. The title summed up the situation: *Ignored and Invisible?* It is all too easy for there to be an unacknowledged competition between professional staff and family carers – with some stereotyping happening here too. For example, I have sometimes heard carers decried as not visiting their relatives in care homes when actually when you talk to them the reason for not visiting is often that it is just too painful both for the care home resident and the carer. This is another area where increased awareness is vital. Given the fact that increasingly people are likely to experience one or more periods of caring in their lives (Henwood et al, 2017), this insight into the experience is very pertinent.

The following chapter is by Anastasia Patrikiou who shares her work on an innovative project funded by the Department of Health and Age UK, which utilised an attachment and person-centred perspective in a moving and nuanced account of psychotherapy with people living with dementia. Her three case studies ably illustrate both the therapeutic work itself and emphasise a point made earlier in her introduction about the need for therapists to own their vulnerability and authenticity to work with people with dementia at relational depth.

Valerie Sinason's reflections on the conference provide an excellent concluding chapter. She ends with some of her poetry which is very fitting and returns us to the world of metaphor and creative arts which can be so important to people with dementia.

As a final note, I would like to leave you, the reader, with a set of questions that puzzle me (Cotter, 2008). What does it mean that our elders are developing memory loss and/or dementia? What does it mean that it is happening to those who have traditionally held the position of the wise in society? What if we have got it wrong and there is some deeper connection between us as human beings through a collective unconscious or a morphic biological resonance – what might the elders be holding for us in society? What might this dis-ease be attempting to balance in society?

References

Alzheimer's Society (2015). *Alzheimer's the greatest concern for over-60s.* Website: https://yougov.co.uk/news/2015/07/26/alzheimers-greatest-concern-over-60s/Accessed on 28th November 2017.

Brown, B. (2010a). *On Vulnerability.* TED Talk. Website: www.ted.com/talks/brene_brown_on_vulnerability. Accessed 28th November 2017.

Brown, B. (2010b). *The Gifts of Imperfection: Let Go of Who You Think You're Supposed to Be and Embrace Who You Are.* Minnesota: Hazelden.

Cotter, A., Fraser, F., Langford, S., & Rose, L. (2001). *Getting Everybody Included.* Report on an action research study exploring the potential of creative arts to enhance communication between people with dementia and staff in long stay settings. London: Magic Me.

Cotter, A. (2008). *Out of Our Minds: Dementia as a Symbol of our Civilisation being in Transition.* London: Guild of Pastoral Psychology.

Eliot, T. S. (1922/1963). *The Wasteland. Collected Poems, 1909–1962.* New York: Harcourt, Brace & World.

Henwood, M. (1998). *Ignored and Invisible? Carers' Experience of the NHS.* Report of a UK research survey. London: Carers National Association.

Henwood M., Larkin M., & Milne A. (2017). *Seeing the Wood for the Trees: Carer-related Research and Knowledge: A Scoping Review.* Social Care Institute for Excellence, Open University, Melanie Henwood Associates. Available online from Social Care Online. Accessed 13th December 2017. http://docs.scie-socialcareonline.org.uk/fulltext/058517.pdf

Jung, C. G. (1951/1966). Fundamental Questions of Psychotherapy. In *The Collected Works Vol. 16: The Practice of Psychotherapy.* 2nd edition. London: Routledge & Kegan Paul.

Kaplan, E. S. (1990). Facing the loss of what makes us uniquely human: Working with dementia patients. In B. Genevay & R. S. Katz (Eds) *Countertransference and Older Clients,* pp. 81–93. London: Sage.

Kitwood, T. (1997). *Dementia Reconsidered: The Person Comes First.* Buckingham: Open University Press.

Menzies-Lyth, I. (1959). The Functioning of Social Systems as a Defence Against Anxiety. *Human Relations, 13,* 95–121.

Sinason, V. (1992, 2010). *Mental Handicap and the Human Condition: An Analytic Approach to Intellectual Disability.* London: Free Association Books.

Sutton, L. (1994). *What is it Like to Lose One's Mind?* Paper presented at the Tenth International Conference of Alzheimer's Disease International. University of Edinburgh.

Chapter 2

Reflections on the film
Ex Memoria (2006)

Josh Appignanesi

The film *Ex Memoria* is based on my grandmother, and her story which was written about by my mother Lisa Appignanesi in her book *Losing The Dead* (1999). Yes, it's a film about dementia, but really it's using dementia to talk about the relationship between the histories we've lived and our memories of them. How we own and recover our pasts, or fail to.

My grandmother was a Polish Jew who lived through the war in Poland and survived, though most of her family did not. I wanted to encode and refer to that history while also making a film that can be read in other more general ways. What all of our memories and histories do to all of us, in the end.

So the idea of beginning the film with a historical trauma or loss wasn't to my mind a theory about "the origin of dementia" except in the broadest sense – that origins are always what dement or unmind us, drive us into madness or reverie, are at the seat of everything, and are what we ultimately return to at the end.

More straightforwardly, when my grandma started to "lose her mind", what she "found" was those earlier parts of her life that had been "lost". She spoke a lot of the brother that literally was lost, went missing in the war (though actually she'd always believed beyond hope that he was alive somewhere, so in a way that was nothing new). And also she returned to speaking Polish, a language she hadn't used for fifty years, which of course I couldn't understand, and my mother only barely.

Trauma is that which repeats despite us, that is, what haunts or returns repeatedly, and as such has the force of madness, of the uncanny, more real than the real. One of the things films can do is go directly to these registers and their quality of association. The moving image has the oneiric power of, for example, a trauma's return (for example, see the double meaning of the term "flashback"). And also because cinema doesn't differentiate necessarily between past, present, future, or dream: everything is happening in the present, all the time. Just like life in which memory and reverie and trauma all appear in the present, mixed up.

So it was out of this soup of ideas that I started. There were two things that struck me as images. One is what it's like being stuck in this chair, in this place, where people can't work out how to communicate with you, and give up, and I wanted to confront the audience with that situation, put them directly in it. But also to be with that face, the face of my gran, which was sort of unreachable to us, unresponsive, and yet in a way closer than any other face because you could really just "be" there with her, looking at her, being looked at, unlike with people who don't have dementia. A bit like the way a close-up in film takes you closer than you'd ever be able to look in real life, and for longer. So the image of just staying with her face came first, I guess you could say a sort of Levinasian idea of this radical encounter with personhood.

Then, going with that face through her memory repeating, bubbling up, in her world, which *does* have a sense but not the sense of the everyday. Bits of the past popping up. Which happens to us all more readily than we normally care to admit, I think, but normally we filter it out. I wanted to take people on that journey in the most sensory and uncanny or haunting way possible, in other words, as it appears in the present.

And in a short film, partly because of how narrative works, a single "trauma" or "backstory" that returns powerfully in later life seemed the best way to approach things. In some ways that's a sleight of hand of course. You're telling a story to an audience. In fact the scene where she thinks she's having her papers checked, were borrowed from my grandfather when "at the end" he lost his mind, due to septicaemia not due to dementia, and thought he was back in Nazi Poland. So I used bits of things, constructed stuff to tell that story.

Originally that was all I wanted to do really, bring the audience into that experience of being with a person who's lost themselves and found themselves in that way. But when I worked with dementia specialists at Bradford Dementia Group, Errolyn Bruce in particular, I learned that you can look at dementia as sort of a code of meanings that can be "broken" or at least encountered properly by people if they're willing to take the time and perceive the person. I thought this was important for people to know and so I changed the script a little bit so that it was clear that there are better ways and worse ways of being with people with dementia. Not negating them or trying to stop them, trying to enter the reality they're currently in, which often comes from their biography, and so on. Obviously her family aren't quite sure what to do with the experience.

The abiding drive to make the film wasn't to instruct about dementia, even though I'm glad it has been used in those contexts and still is. For me as a filmmaker it was about this very intimate but very alienating encounter with a woman who had a very different past to me, one that feels to me completely inaccessible and yet very powerful at the same time – a bit like a trauma! Perhaps this is what transgenerational haunting is. You could say it's an effort to understand that, and hence to express or memorialise the experience of this passing generation whose trauma defined the European century and who now are all soon to be gone.

References

Appignanesi, J. (2006). *Ex Memoria*. Writer and Director, Josh Appignanesi. Missing In Action Films.
Appignanesi, L. (1999). *Losing The Dead*. London: Chatto & Windus.

Ex Memoria

A film by Josh Appignanesi
Starring:
  Sara Kestelman
  Shaun Dooley
  Natalie Press
  Julie LeGrand
  David Birkin

See it here:
https://vimeo.com/133611676
password: Wellcome

Official Selection at festivals including: Edinburgh, Montreal, Melbourne, LA Shorts, Jerusalem, Hamptons, Brief Encounters, Bilbao, Riverrun and Dinard Festival. Kodak BAFTA Runner-Up 2006–7

  Written and directed by Josh Appignanesi
  Produced by Mia Bays
  Director of Photography Nanu Segal
  Production Designer Erik Rehl
  Editor Nicolas Gaster
  Costume Designer Anushia Nieradzik
  Sound Recordist Patrick Owen
  Casting by Lucy Townsend and Julie Harkin
  Sound Designer Joakim Sundstrom
  Line Producer Joanna Gueritz
  Production Manager Magali Gibert
  Executive Producers Sandy Lieberson, Errollyn Bruce
  A Missing In Action Films Production
  Developed in association with the Bradford Dementia Group
  Funded by Wellcome Trust

www.joshappignanesi.com
@JoshAppFilm
16 mins

Chapter 3

Lipstick

Sara Kestelman

On the day my mother died
I slipped my arms
into her cardigan –
black wool mixed with silk
her favourite
on her small frame serving as a coat –
and on my lips
the lipstick from her bag,
her lips on mine
and so for every day since
until the summer robs me
of the extra layer
and the lipstick is no more.

Sara Kestelman, May 1997

Chapter 4

An attachment approach to understanding and living well with dementia

Kate White

The inspiration for accepting the invitation to contribute to the groundbreaking conference in 2014 arose from several factors coming together in both my personal and professional life. My main motivation has come from the discoveries my partner and I have made together arising from his diagnosis of Alzheimer's some nine years ago in 2009. This has led us both to a more profound understanding of the central importance of our attachment relationship as we navigate our shared experiences of this new phase in our lives with all its challenges. In addition, it has given a renewed focus and recognition of the simplicity and brilliance of John Bowlby's work as we see its applications in this field personally and professionally. Attachment theory is our shared secure base for exploration and soothing in times of both turmoil and joy and I want to share my thoughts with you. It is moving to bring together these different parts of my life experience now that I'm in my sixties! I owe a great deal to a fellow contributor to this book, Pam Schweitzer, and I feel honoured to have got to know her. She has been a remarkable and wonderful influence in my life in the last few years personally and professionally since John and I met her as participants on her extraordinary and innovatory project called *Remembering Yesterday Caring Today*. This is a group for people living with dementia and their families, which I can honestly say was transformative for my partner and I and for others in our group. More about that in her chapter.

The aim of this chapter is to explore the particular needs and vulnerabilities of those who are living with dementia through the unique lens of attachment theory. I will discuss, with examples, how people with dementia, who are often marginalised and impacted by loss of memory, can be empowered by participation, together with their family carers, in reminiscence groups. Here we see in action a relationship-based intervention which is unique, and I think works so brilliantly because it is underpinned by understanding that we need a dyadic intervention to support the person *and* their carer to find new ways of being together. I will also be discussing the potential of using another group for dyads called the *Circle of Security*, devised by Bob Marvin and his colleagues in their work with parents and children.

Figure 4.1 John and the birds of love

With my experiences as both a professional caregiver and as a family member I will be looking at the way dementia raises fears of disappearing connections in us all. I want to explore the ways we can, as a community, learn about how revisiting and sharing the different stages in our life stories and attachment histories can lead to deepening intimacy and the renewal of emotional bonds with the creation of new meanings.

> One day after breakfast we (John and Julia, his companion for the day) were walking across the Heath we spotted a tree full of birds twittering madly. As John is very good at communicating with birds I asked him what they might be tweeting.
> "They are saying 'I love you and for god's sake don't leave me!!!'"

This story brings our everyday attachment needs into the picture immediately.
In a recent interview John was asked by David Sheard:

> "How does it feel John when your memory isn't working as well as it should?" I was seated next to him and we were holding hands – my heart was racing in anticipation of his reply. . .

Without a moment's hesitation he replied:
"I feel fear – frightened because you don't know where you are or what's happening next. . .."
"What helps you at those times?"
"Love – support, friends and neighbours."

We were all in tears – John had summarised it all with such eloquence. Emotionally he has such an accurate perception – and as I have learned with him over these years it is emotions that you need to communicate with not cognitions and words, especially with this illness (Sheard, 2013).

Here he puts at the centre of our lives our common need for **love and relationship.**

Relationship-centred interventions

I want to argue that what is needed in the situation where someone is living with dementia is an approach which is relationship centred so both the person with dementia and their family carer are offered an opportunity as a couple to renew, recover and revitalise their attachment relationship which, under the strain of this diagnosis and the caregiving role, may have become fractured and estranged. Intimacy may have become lost amidst exhaustion and fear.

I will be describing two such interventions and will illustrate from attachment theory principles why I think that they are successful. I describe each in summary below.

Reminiscence work involving the dyadic relationship of carer and cared for together

This group, which meets over twelve weeks, involves expanding into and sharing in the stories of peoples' lives; rebuilding memory and identity of self with others; building up self-esteem and rekindling a capacity for joy and vitality recognition; witnessing and dissolving shame whilst encouraging a narrative coherence of each participant's life story.

The Circle of Security approach (Powell et al., 2016) derives from a group intervention devised for parents and their children, which has been developed to enhance and empower more sensitive and attuned responsiveness in caregivers to the attachment cues of their children. It is my contention that a dyadic intervention of this kind might be used to support carers who perhaps have insecure attachment patterns from their childhoods thus are dismissing or preoccupied in their way of being with the cared for person. These ways of responding are not optimal and can lead to a cycle of fear and anxiety that is difficult, for both caregiver and the person being cared for, to pull back from.

Attachment theory

In this next section I will begin by outlining the basic tenets of attachment theory.

Relationship is of course central – this comes as no surprise. I feel Arietta Slade (2008) expresses this beautifully in this quote:

> We survive by forming relationships, and adapting to the minds *and the bodies* of others [my addition in italics]. **Relationships are the remedy for fear** – of loss, of annihilation, of psychic emptiness – and offer us the deepest expression of our humanity.

In her beautiful language, the poet Adrienne Rich (1977) writes:

> That creatures must find each other for bodily comfort
> That voices of the psyche drive through the flesh
> Further than the dense brain could have foretold,
> That the planetary nights are growing cold for those
> On the same journey who want to touch
> One creature-traveller clear to the end;
> That without tenderness, we are in hell.

These two quotes for me summarise the essence of what we are talking about when we refer to our need for attachment relationships. There is of course a systemic complexity involved when the attachment patterns of different individuals come into play with each other.

Person with dementia, family carer and professional carer

In this triad of the person with dementia, family carer and professional carer are the intersecting systems of attachment with reciprocal caregiving/care seeking, exploration, interest sharing and the sexual and affiliative systems (Heard et al. 2009). The fear system may intrude into any of the above network of relationships and create anxiety and distortions in understanding the patterns of communication and associated feelings.

In addition, *all* of these interactions are taking place in a social environment and a context of external power dynamics, which contribute positively or negatively to the sense of safety. For example, a lack of support either financial or practical can impact on each person's capacity to respond with compassion and/or empathy when under stress.

In the situation many of us encounter there are these intersecting systems. When living with dementia the individual, like my partner John, is embedded in several systems at once; his own internal working model of attachment with its history in attachment relationships as a child and as an adult; the same components in me, his partner and family caregiver intersecting with him, and both of our attachment patterns are then aroused in relation to any professional caregiver we then encounter, such as our GP, or nurse from the memory service. I have tried to represent this in the triadic diagram in Figure 4.2.

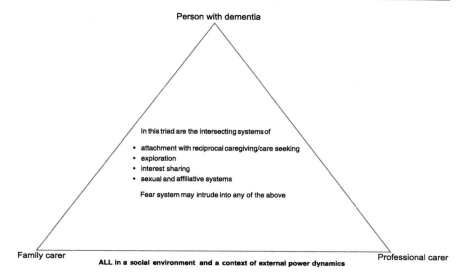

Person with dementia

In this triad are the intersecting systems of

- attachment with reciprocal caregiving/care seeking
- exploration
- interest sharing
- sexual and affiliative systems

Fear system may intrude into any of the above

Family carer

ALL in a social environment and a context of external power dynamics

Professional carer

Figure 4.2

Key concepts from attachment theory

These include:

- Attachment
- Reciprocal careseeking and caregiving
- Emotional co-regulation of fear states
- Secure base and safe haven
- Separation anxiety
- Exploration
- Narrative coherence
- Loss and mourning

These concepts are central in our understanding of what I am calling "Relationship centred interventions"; however, in this chapter I am going to focus on just three:

- Attachment
- Secure base and safe haven
- Separation anxiety

John Bowlby, the founder of attachment theory, defines attachment as follows:

> Intimate attachments to other human beings are the hub around which a person's life revolves, not only when he is an infant or a toddler or a schoolchild but throughout his adolescence and his years of maturity as well, and on into old age.
>
> (Bowlby, 1980, p. 422)

> Attachment is any form of behaviour that results in a person attaining and maintaining proximity to some other clearly identified figure who is conceived as better able to cope with the world. It is most obvious when a person is frightened, fatigued, or sick and is assuaged by comforting and caregiving.
>
> (Bowlby, 1988, pp. 26–27)

Attachment is linked to the human response to *fear* and is most clearly evident when there are threats of separation or actual separation and abandonment.

Think of those scenes where a parent who is out shopping but is now desperate to get their child home and eventually says things like "I'm going to leave you here – byeee. . ." Here the fear system will be flooding the child's aroused attachment system and the combination will bring the child running and maybe crying, trying to catch up to avoid the terror of being left alone. We see the two systems involved in an attachment relationship working together, namely care seeking and reciprocally caregiving. The careseeker maintains and secures the attention of the caregiver by:

- Smiling
- Vocalising
- Crying
- Following

Attention and proximity to the attachment figure is ensured through these behaviours.

The person with cognitive and memory difficulties is likely to be experiencing fear and anxiety as particular familiar environments become an unsafe place and disorientation undermines confidence and felt safety. The behaviours described above may be used to find the safety they are desperate to experience. So, we might be in a position to understand as caregivers why a person is crying out to find us when we might just be in the next room or following in our footsteps around the house to keep us in view. These are all, according to Bowlby, attachment-seeking behaviours.

The aim of the attachment system in states of arousal is to find safety with an attachment figure, so the person will start seeking out their attachment figure who may be a parent or partner but in the case of someone with dementia could be a professional carer in the nursing home or the daughter with whom they are now living.

When afraid it is through attaining proximity with "a preferred other" who will provide us with protection and affect regulation that we can then regain a feeling state of safety and thus assuaged we are able to return to exploring our environment once more.

Think back to a recent experience of your own – perhaps you got locked out of your home on your own or broke down in your car on the motorway or missed the last train home – think about the fear and what you did to assuage it.

As we grow older the physical presence of our primary attachment figure is often not required as we can go "inside" metaphorically to find soothing of our fears from within. We have internalised the attachment relationship and now can soothe and calm ourselves.

We have developed what is known as an "internal working model" and in the case of secure attachment we have come to understand ourselves as lovable and capable of loving others because we have been exposed to repeated and sufficient responsiveness and attuned soothing for us to internalise this feeling. If we haven't had the attuned responsiveness to our attachment needs, we can develop insecure attachment. A preoccupied state of mind develops if the attunement to our needs has been intermittent so we are left in the hope and longing for more. Consequently, we are left with a feeling we are not lovable and worthy of attention and think if only we tried harder we would finally get what we long for. We try harder by showing our feelings a lot in the hope we will be responded to and sometimes we are, which keeps us ever on the lookout and hopeful so we stay very close. We then may be accused of being "clingy" by those who don't understand our internal terror and desperation for reassuring connection and love.

If our needs for soothing have been constantly rebuffed, we begin to understand that we have to hide our attachment needs for love and soothing, so we might have to appear competent and self-reliant so as to be able to remain in proximity to our caregivers by never asking for what we really need or showing our vulnerability. This latter way of surviving deprivation of this kind is known as avoidant or dismissing attachment.

The attachment behavioural system

Figure 4.3 summarises the key features of attachment theory and shows how insecure attachment develops in response to the various ways caregivers respond to the cues from those seeking care. It also shows how repeated responses develop into patterns of defence and protection.

"Secure Base" and "Safe Haven"

Mary Ainsworth was John Bowlby's primary research collaborator and coined the terms Secure Base and Safe Haven.

Initially a primary attachment figure provides the secure base for the child – attachment behaviour is responded to, feelings co-regulated and assuaged thus exploration can begin.

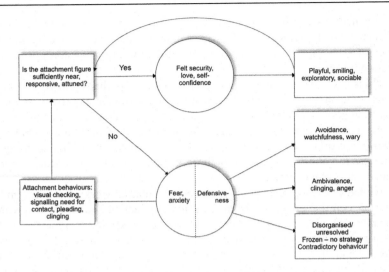

Figure 4.3 The attachment behavioural system adapted from Jeremy Holmes

Secure attachment relationships arise from repeated experiences of attuned, available, consistent caregiving responses to the child's careseeking behaviour.

The child, if all goes well enough, develops an internalised secure base from which to explore and a safe internal haven to which she can return symbolically for comfort and the assuaging of fear states.

Our secure base is understood as the place, emotionally, where the attachment system when assuaged is "switched off" so enabling the potential for exploration – internal and literally externally. The safe haven is the emotional and often literal place provided by an attachment figure that the child returns to for refuelling during exploration if this becomes scary or in some way overwhelming to continue. In a secure attachment relationship, the child's need to return to their safe haven is welcomed and affirmed rather than ridiculed or rebuffed by their caregiver.

Erik Hesse and Mary Main (Hesse & Main, 2000, p.1106) identify very helpfully for us what they term as the caregiver's secure base behaviours. These are described as providing "scaffolding", namely support for the attachment relationship through the following kinds of activities:

• Identifying clear and familiar routines and plans for the day
• Supporting exploration with information
• Preparing for new experiences
• Attuning to emotional states
• Reviewing and reminiscing about the day, photos, stories, music
• Balancing between the person's attachment system and exploratory system

It is my contention that where dementia starts to encroach, my sense is the "internalised secure base" and "internalised safe haven" are eroded and the person is no longer able to assuage their own fear states and needs to have an external secure base and haven of safety to be able to feel safe and oriented in the world. The caregiver needs to provide, in many different ways, the scaffolding for the relationship, which has become fragile and tenuous through different erosions of safety arising from the dementia.

It is clear to me that this experience of deterioration in the person being cared for is too much for any one person, so the caregiver needs to feel the support of family and community to continue to provide a secure base as it can be tiring and exhausting to offer this "scaffolding" literally twenty-four hours a day for seven days a week. Fear states can also be flooding and disorienting, and caregivers can find themselves, in the countertransference, muddled, confused, frightened, angry and overwhelmed as well.

The story below by Gemma Jones (2011), illustrates beautifully some of the points I've been making about the usefulness of an "attachment lens" through which to see and understand the sometimes confusing and overwhelming behaviour of people who are living with dementia and who may be very frightened and thus frighten others by what is happening to them.

A story of a person living with dementia by Gemma Jones

Re-surfacing traumas not leaving people alone with fears and tears

People with dementia who are disoriented-in-time (unaware of their age, where they are living, how old they or their family members are, cannot recall who is alive and deceased), sometimes re-experience past situations as if they were occurring again (Miesen, 1995, 1999; Jones et al., 2006a, 2006b). The "triggers" for re-experienced events are not necessarily predictable but have included, physical sensations, the presence of specific objects, darkness, mis-perceiving cues in the environment, and perhaps most importantly – picking up on an unpleasant and impersonal "emotional atmosphere".

There are a variety of such experiences, but by far the most familiar examples involve elderly residents in care home settings, who think they are young again and are feeling unsafe, who tell staff they "want to go home" to their parents, spouse or other close attachment figure. [When people with dementia are disoriented-in-time and say they want to go home, in the first instance this is understood as their expression of feelings of fear and discomfort, rather than as a literal request to return to a previous actual abode.] Some residents eventually think they are "at home" with their parents (or at work) and then stop requesting to go there.

Dr. Bère Miesen spent many years studying the progression of changes leading to people with dementia speaking about deceased parents as if they are still alive. This led him to write about the importance of not leaving people with dementia who are disoriented-in-time, alone. Also, encouraging caregivers to be visibly present as much as possible so people do not become lost and distressed in their search for finding a "safe other person" to be with.

This also applies to people with dementia in their own home settings. Family carers sometimes say the person behaves like their "shadow" or a "puppy" that will not leave them alone, even to go to the next room.

One of Miesen's conclusions was that people with dementia who cannot "find safety" [feel safe] by staying near people who symbolise "safe, significant people from the past" [attachment figures], only have one remaining way to feel safe. That is to try to remember [search for and re-live memories of] feeling/being safe with them.

This implies that people with dementia try to "problem-solve", and actively "search for safety and comfort" – however they do so within the limitations of their damaged cognitive abilities. To new caregiving staff, such time-dislocated situations can seem bizarre and inappropriate. If staff don't understand what's happening to a resident, they may respond literally to the facts, sometimes unhelpfully.

For example, an 80-year-old lady with dementia residing in a nursing home had been straining on the toilet for about fifteen minutes, without effect. She then suddenly started shouting loudly and repeatedly calling out for help saying, *"please, please, help, someone, help – the baby's coming"*.

Two young women staff members were the first to answer the summons, neither of whom had experienced childbirth. They laughed, telling her "the facts":

- She was 87
- She wasn't pregnant
- She couldn't be pregnant or have a baby at her age
- She was "just on the toilet having a bowel movement"

Though they stated the facts, they had missed the feelings and sensations – and had either not noticed that this lady was frightened and uncomfortable, or didn't know how to respond to this. [Their intervention is an example of the inappropriate use of old-style "reality orientation" with a person with dementia who is disoriented-in-time.] The lady seemed to completely ignore their responses, and continued shouting as before.

Eventually, an experienced caregiver arrived, and more helpfully said:

"I'm here to help you. I'll stay with you. Tell me where it hurts."
"Down below," the lady replied.
"In your bottom?"
"Yes," the lady said.
"Is it a feeling of pressure?"
"Yes, the baby's coming soon," the lady said.
"It feels like the pressure of having a baby?"
"Yes," the lady shouted.
"You're frightened."
"Yes, please don't leave me," she whispered.
"I won't leave you. Let's see what will make you more comfortable."

The caregiver stayed with her. The lady stopped calling out, but her moaning continued another ten minutes, without any results. The caregiver helped the lady to bed and arranged for someone to examine her. She was severely constipated and required a stool softener and several enemas. Only then did she stop talking about "the baby coming". [Although this lady had children, there was no documentation about whether her deliveries had been long, difficult or otherwise traumatic – but the link between the physical sensation of rectal pressure/discomfort and childbirth is certainly a familiar and plausible one, despite her dislocation-in-time.]

The above situation lasted only a day but occasionally, associations of former turbulence and trauma are recurrent or very persistent – some occur daily for months on end. They are upsetting to everyone around, and usually result in a person being isolated from others, to minimise the distress and disruption to the communal atmosphere.

[To my knowledge, the frequency of such situations has not been researched; neither has the range and order of the care planning interventions used, been suitably documented and analysed. In my experience, staff are upset that they do not know what to do to help people, do not document it well, and avoid discussing it; they see it as a failure to care well, or to be able to comfort someone, on their part.]

Miesen's (1999) work identified several patterns of distress linked to people being disoriented-in-time:

- distress which disappears for the duration that another remains present
- distress which disappears during and for some time after a person has been present
- (and rarely) distress which is resistant to disappearing, or does not disappear, even in the presence of others

[Miesen suggests that some people have been so badly hurt in life, and not healed from the pain and sorrow sufficiently, to trust anyone anymore.]

Next, is an example of some intensive, longer-term care planning that staff tried with a lady; it changed her "type c" persistent distress, into "type a".

A lady (I'll call her Alice), aged 84, had dementia and lived in a nursing home. All day long, she alternately cried and called out for her mother; "Where are you mummy?" "Please come mummy" and "Why don't you come mummy?"

Alice had been doing this virtually all day, every day, for months (since her transfer from a residential care home) – despite all the best efforts of everyone to engage with her, distract her, comfort her, and try to change her mood. In the morning she had visible tears; but even though they seemed to run out as the day continued, her crying didn't. Various types of medication had been tried, unsuccessfully; since the crying and calling out continued the medication was stopped. Staff were then told that there was nothing that could be done for her, her behaviour was a consequence of "the dementia".

Staff could not readily get eye contact with Alice, let alone get her to join in any activities or groups. She was unable to answer the caregiving staff or her fellow residents when they enquired about "What was the matter", "Why are you so upset?", and "What can we do to help you?" In spite of the efforts of various residents to comfort her, she did not stop calling out and crying; some mistook her for a frightened child. When nothing they did consoled her, they didn't want to sit near her and asked for her to be quieted ["shut her up"] and removed. Alice's distress quickly spread to all present and made the atmosphere in the room tense. (Staff could not recall Alice ever having had a visitor since being admitted; perhaps her family/contacts were similarly upset, and could not bear the pain of seeing her distress repeatedly.)

Staff were at their wits end as to what else to try. (Providing full-time, one-to-one care for Alice was not an option for financial staffing reasons.) With no other obvious solution, the decision was made to keep the lounge area pleasant for the other residents. This meant keeping Alice in her bedroom for large portions of the day, so others would not hear her shouting and crying and become agitated too. Not surprisingly, her bedroom was at the end of a corridor, furthest from the lounge.

Then, a new life-history event came to light, one that stimulated further thinking. When Alice was 7 years old, her mother had died whilst trying to help the neighbours, whose house was on fire. Alice completed her schooling and seemed to have led a "normal" life – she married, was a homemaker, had children, grandchildren, and hobbies – there was no knowledge of particular ill health or any mental health difficulties in her life. Her dementia had been progressing slowly after being first noticed some years earlier. Whether Alice's grieving for her mother's death was "incomplete", and who supported her at that time, was not known.

In light of Miesen's (1995, 1999) work (above), it was considered that perhaps, in seeking "memories of safety with her mother", Alice had returned to a distant "crisis memory" – recalling wanting her mother, calling for her, but mother never returning. This possibility, prompted a group of staff members to think about trying to create the "feeling of safety" for Alice.

Several caregiving staff were particularly distressed at her behaviour. With new motivation they decided to try to see if giving Alice extra intervals of close one-to-one contact in her bedroom would help (in addition to the time spent giving her routine personal care and assistance with nourishment). They voluntarily gave up their coffee and lunch breaks, in turn, to be with her. Their goal was to get increased eye contact and reduce the crying and calling out, even for a few minutes. They greeted her, sat close to Alice, looked at her, held her hand/s, and spoke/sang to her. "I'm. . . ., I'm here to be with you . . . I'd like to tell you about. . . . and sing something for you. You probably know this. You can join in if you'd like."

After several days, when she seemed accustomed to this contact, a caregiver tried putting an arm around her. Alice did not resist. The caregiver started making slow, rocking movements, and humming a lullaby to her; she seemed comforted. Alice stopped crying during some of these intervals. This result was the incentive that staff needed to continue their "voluntary" work with her. Progress continued patiently.

Alice's improvement also meant that staff could sit in the lounge with her for increasing intervals, (rather than in her bedroom). Within two months Alice had stopped calling out for her mother as much, and, surprisingly, had started to look for "her children". [This was seen as a significant change, because it indicated that she was also remembering her role as a mother – who gave comfort – rather than as a child – in need of comfort].

Alice remained disoriented-in-time, but her crying stopped for the most part, except for occasional episodes. It was now possible for her to sit in the lounge and to be present at various activities there. Although she did not join in, she seemed to be pleased to be present, and observing quietly.

(It is worth noting that given that they had been told there was "nothing that could be done for Alice", some members of staff did not see the purpose of giving up their break time, so participating in this intervention was on a voluntary basis at first. The result of this intervention, in this instance, was a positive one. Nancy Feil (2002) gives another example of reaching someone who was thought to be "unreachable" because of dementia.)

Thinking back over thirty years, I recall half a dozen examples of such "extremely distressed residents" in care homes in Canada, France, the Netherlands and the UK; I still wonder if a similar sort of intervention would have helped them also.

In discussing such examples with course participants, a number of them have become concerned about how past traumatic event/s in their own life might "re-surface" in later life, or if they get dementia. They don't want to think about them now, let alone re-live them over and over again later.

Their question can be rephrased as: How do we heal from the psychological hurts in life (the consequences of betrayals, disasters, abuses, and accidents) so that they don't keep hurting?

No one gets through life unscathed, but some people are deeply and multiply hurt. The old advice still applies – in general terms – don't keep it buried inside; speak to a wise, trusted friend. If that isn't sufficient or possible, there are many sources of specialist services available nowadays, including counselling, peer-support and therapy – for specific types of help. This wasn't so for those people who are old, and in our care now.

The key message for trying to bring comfort to someone with dementia, who is frightened (and other people in life), is to let them know: "*You are not alone – I'm staying with you.*" This message can be given in many forms, verbally and non-verbally, and through every sense.

In dementia care, you will often be working to allay "fear behaviour". Considering that most "anger behaviour" has its roots in fear, it is even more important to learn to work well to allay fear.

Gemma Jones' account has many links to the work of David Sheard and Sally Knocker whose training for those caring for people with dementia focuses on the importance of tuning into feelings, creating connection, engagement and a sense of belonging. Known as "The Butterfly Approach" (Sheard, 2012, 2013 & 2018 and Knocker, 2015, 2018), their work has transformed and revolutionised our understanding of what matters most in compassionate dementia care.

Attachment and separation anxiety

Having described Alice's story, we can understand it as a separation response reactivated from the past – displaced in time as Bowlby (1988) would say.

Separation anxiety is experienced when our attachment system is activated but cannot be shut off or terminated by the presence or behaviour of a specific person to whom we are attached literally or symbolically. Our aim is to remain organised – having a strategy to survive and not disintegrate during separations – in spite of being emotionally dysregulated.

Separation

John Bowlby quotes James Robertson, one of his research collaborators, who describes the experience of a young child during separation in a most articulate way:

> If a child is taken from his mother's care at this age *(at the age of two, sic)*, when he is so possessively and passionately attached to her, it is indeed as if his world has been shattered. His intense need of her is unsatisfied, and the frustration and longing may send him frantic with grief. It takes an exercise of imagination to sense the intensity of this distress. He is as overwhelmed as any adult who has lost a beloved person by death. To the child of two with his lack of understanding and complete inability to tolerate frustration it is really as if his mother had died. He does not know death, but only absence; and if the only person who can satisfy his imperative need is absent, she might as well be dead, so overwhelming is his sense of loss.
>
> (Bowlby, 1980, p. 17)

Separation response

This response is characterised by three phases identified in the original research by James Robertson and his partner Joyce:

1   Protest – related to separation anxiety

  • anger of hope to get carer back

2   Despair – related to grief and mourning

- anger of despair
- state of disorganisation

3   Detachment – related to defences

- denial of wish for relationship and reorganising around the person's absence

These were the patterns that their meticulous research work confirmed (Robertson & Robertson, 1989). The person's initial response to separation is characterised by protest – crying out for the loved person to return and provide comfort and safety, thus soothing the attachment cry. In Bowlby's words expressing the "anger of hope" the hope of regaining the soothing presence of the one who is loved (Bowlby, 1973, p. 245).

After time has elapsed with no return of the comforting attachment figure, the person becomes increasingly despairing, losing hope and entering a phase of anger, grief and deep mourning for the loss of the person upon whom they have relied for comfort and whom they require to enable a return to any semblance of emotional equilibrium. Bowlby described the anger expressed at this stage as being the "anger of despair" – no hope of return now. This point is characterised by a gradual descent into a "state of disorganisation". No longer searching, but emotionally disintegrating.

The final stage is one of detachment – a protection from the searing anguish and harrowing sorrow of loss. Here there are a variety of emotional defences one of which is characterised by denial, denial of the wish and longing for a relationship of comfort for the time being.

Here begins a gradual and painful process of reconfiguring one's life around the attachment figure's absence. In childhood we can see children adapting themselves to the loss of a parent in imaginative but agonisingly painful ways: perhaps flinging themselves into their studies – excelling at school or gaining recognition through sporting or musical prowess. Alternatively becoming focused on controlling their emotional states by an embodiment of their pain through self-harm, and distressed eating.

Finding an empathic response to those with dementia is I think enhanced and enabled through an understanding of the fear of separation and actual separation as described above.

Reunion

It is said that the separation response is the test of an attachment bond. We can see that bond coming alive with clarity, as if emerging out of the mist, when we witness the ecstatic embrace of lovers or parents and children after a time apart.

Mary Ainsworth's "Strange Situation Test"

Mary Ainsworth's breakthrough was to take her naturalistic home observations of attachment relationships and the children's responses to separations from their caregivers and subsequent reunions, which she had noticed varied in very particular ways, and devise a research tool called the "Strange Situation Test".

Reunion behaviour, as it is rather unpoetically called, reveals the child's (or adult's) internal working model of their attachment relationship. The person's pattern of response upon reunion with their attachment figure is coded carefully to then provide a window into the different and distinctive attachment patterns, secure, ambivalent, avoidant or disorganised with respect to their attachment figure.

Reunion behaviour in people living with dementia and their daughters

Howard Steele's (Steele et al., 2004) research in relation to the reunion behaviour of mothers living with dementia and their daughters is an application of Ainsworth's work on separation as the test of the quality of an attachment bond. This study looked at a group of daughters with different attachment patterns to their mothers. Those who provided a coherent account of their attachment history assessed using the Adult Attachment Interview (i.e. they showed secure states of mind) were more likely to be met on reunion with their mothers with signs of joy and proximity seeking by their mothers with dementia in the adapted strange situation test. This remained the case despite the severity of the dementia. It was also found that there was careseeking behaviour – searching for contact and connection – even in late stages of dementia. The researchers concluded that this demonstrated the secure internal working models of the mothers with secure attachment patterns – revealing internal messages such as "I am worthy of being loved/the other is likely to be available and responsive" – were still present.

I have included here an extract from their research report (Steele, Phibbs, & Woods, 2004) as I feel it communicates this so well in their own words.

> We hypothesized that greater evidence of coherence in the daughters' interviews would correlate with greater evidence of joyfulness in their mothers upon reunion. This would be so, we expected, because daughters unhindered by emotional conflicts stemming from their attachment histories would be more emotionally available to their declining mothers, and their mothers would reflect this state of affairs by showing joy and relatedness upon reunion. Conversely, we expected that low coherence in the daughters' interviews, stemming from ongoing emotional difficulties rooted in their past attachment histories, would be correlated with diminished levels of joy in their mothers upon reunion. Drawing on the compelling anecdotal evidence of emotional responsiveness and core selfhood, even if nonverbal, surviving into the latest stages of dementia (e.g., Kitwood, 1997a,b), we further anticipated that

the intergenerational results we expected would hold, even after taking into account the severity of dementia in the mother.

The more coherent the daughter was in the AAI, the more likely the mother was to score highly on the cumulative index of joy and relatedness upon reunion. The estimated shared variance between these daughter and mother attachment variables is over forty percent, with the severity of the mothers' dementia being unrelated to whether they were joyful or not upon reunion.

This suggests that unresolved grief in a daughter makes it much less likely that a mother with dementia will respond positively upon reunion, even if their advanced stage of dementia has perhaps led them to feel acutely distressed by the separation, and prone to seek out the daughter upon reunion.

Daughters whose interviews were more organised and believable with respect to childhood experiences, and more emotionally balanced and valuing of attachment – regardless of whether the interview was judged insecure overall – had mothers who responded toward them with greater joy and interest.

Mothers' severity of dementia did not relate significantly to their reunion behaviour. In other words, there were some very animated and positive emotional responses upon reunion, even from some of those mothers with severe dementia.

Daughters with impoverished levels of coherence, or heightened levels of unresolved mourning, had mothers who were significantly less joyful and less related upon reunion. Furthermore, this intergenerational association was unrelated to the severity of dementia in the mother.

Most importantly, the severity of their dementia in our sample was not found to be associated with their joyful facial expressiveness, proximity seeking, contact maintaining, overall responsiveness, and overall attunement with their daughters on reunion in the modified strange situation. In other words, some women who were very advanced in the disease process were nonetheless very responsive to their daughters. This highlights the need to appreciate how a core sense of self, capable of responding socially and emotionally to a preferred other, survives into the very late stages of the disease, if not until the end itself. This observation is consistent with neurobiological evidence and speculation on areas of preservation within the brain function of the person with dementia. It may be that what survives longest are certain core features of what was encoded and stored earliest, namely one's earliest internal working model of attachment arguably established in the right orbital frontal cortex (see Schore, 2000). Certainly, appreciation for the social and emotional self within the person with dementia is growing (e.g., Kitwood, 1997a; Sabat, 2001), and there is evidence of such attachment-informed knowledge positively influencing clinical interventions, social policy and practice concerning the needs of people with dementia and their carers (Miesen, 2002).

The results also provide some indications that daughters who were more resolved regarding past loss or trauma, and who demonstrated higher evidence of reflective functioning, also contributed positively to the likelihood of their mothers showing trusting, animated interest, and joy upon reunion.

The life-long significance of reunion behaviour following a separation from a loved one, on whom we feel dependent, is underscored by these findings. Inhibited responses upon reunion by the older person with dementia may be seen in this context as an indication of "excess disability" (Reifler & Larson, 1990) reflecting a malignant pattern of relating to the daughter such that the mother with dementia is appearing more disabled than the extent of any brain pathology would indicate ought to be the case. This is consistent with the views expressed in Clare and Woods (2001) on how rehabilitation efforts with people with dementia should include as a central aim the reduction of excess disability, taking into consideration the family interactions of the person with dementia. The current work points to the immense value of attachment theory and research methods in further understanding and supporting people with dementia, and those they depend on for care.

My comment on this research is that the daughters with secure attachment states of mind would be able to ask for the practical and emotional help and support they needed in times of distress so providing practical ways in which their environment might be contributing to their capacity for maintaining an attuned and responsive relationship to the mother they are now caring for. I can confirm that now, as a person with earned security but with a history of an insecure avoidant state of mind, I might at times waver in asking for what I need in way of support but know that when I am properly supported, for example getting sufficient sleep, then I am able to be more attuned to my partner's fears and needs as well as participate in his joyful exuberance for life and connection. So, with secure attachment comes the entitlement to perhaps demand an environment of shared care – hence my commitment to writing about the injustices of the hidden needs of unpaid carers. There are 670,000 of us in the UK and we are saving our economy an estimated eleven billion a year (Carers Trust, 2017).

It is shocking.

There are 850,000 people with dementia in the UK. It is one of the main causes of disability later in life, ahead of cancer, cardiovascular disease and stroke. As a country we spend much less on dementia than on these other conditions (Alzheimer's Society, 2017).

Secure attachment and memory difficulties

In another study (Perren et al., 2007) people living with dementia but with a secure attachment history showed the following responses:

- More positive emotion, joy and interest
- Better emotional regulation
- Increased sociability
- Less anger and fear and shyness
- Their carers felt less burdened

Perhaps an internal experience of secure attachment enabled people in this group to accept being cared for and benefit from comforting and therefore with their attachment needs soothed and met they were then able to explore the environment and relationships with more confidence and less anxiety.

It would be interesting to discover whether those with "earned security" – that is those who have perhaps, either through attuned care from grandparents, a wise choice of life partner or effective psychotherapy, resolved early attachment trauma and are thus able to enter into new relationships and explore the world with interest and confidence despite the memory difficulties and anxiety associated with dementia.

Insecure attachment and dementia

The same study described above found that those who were living with dementia and who also had insecure attachment states of mind showed the following characteristics:

- More day and night disturbances in those with a dismissing attachment pattern
- Increased depression and anxiety in those who had a preoccupied attachment pattern
- Increased agitation and aggression was found in people with dementia where carers themselves had an insecure attachment dismissing pattern – my comment here is that maybe they were unable to provide a secure base or soothe because of their own history so limiting their capacity to remain emotionally regulated and not feeling entitled to ask for support
- If the caregiver had a dismissing attachment pattern it was more likely that the person being cared for would be institutionalised

These observations make sense in the context of understanding the internal emotional state of both caregiver and care seeker. I hasten to add that the caregivers' responses are likely to be additionally affected by how much sleep they have had and whether they are enabled, through support from the community and health and social services, to lead a wide-ranging life of their own whilst having caregiving responsibilities. There are three eight-hour shifts in a day. This level of care is very demanding and exhausting physically and emotionally.

Relationship centred interventions

I will turn now to the interventions that, in my view, are effective because they are based on attachment principles and involve both carer and cared for together by offering the possibility of lasting relational change.

The first is the project *Remembering Yesterday and Caring Today* (RYCT) which is primarily reminiscence work involving the dyadic relationship of carer and cared for together and has been pioneered by Pam Schweitzer and her European Reminiscence Network colleagues (Schweitzer & Bruce, 2008). It is a remarkable innovation that is written about more fully in chapter 8.

In brief the structure of the twelve-week intervention is as follows:

> We hold a series of two-hour sessions following the life course of people with dementia and their carers. We use reminiscence and creative approaches to help everyone express themselves. It is a programme which aims to include the person with dementia **and** their caregiver and therefore impacts upon their relationship, most often in a very positive way.

The programme provides the opportunity for:

- Expanding, sharing in the stories of peoples' lives
- Rebuilding memory and identity of self with others
- Building up self-esteem and capacity for joy and "vitality recognition" (Stern, 2010)
- Witnessing and dissolving shame
- Encouraging a narrative coherence of their life story

What the RYCT groups do is to provide opportunities within a safe space for those caring and those being cared for to re attune to one another through experiencing dynamic "now moments" as described by Daniel Stern (Stern, 2004) which shift the dyadic relationship into a new level of more attuned responsiveness. An example of this was at the end of the RYCT group where we were asked to prepare an "appreciation" of our cared for person's qualities – namely what we treasured and loved about them. The person we care for was also invited to do the same and we were all supported by the staff and volunteers to prepare something. This was a most moving and extraordinary moment magnified by listening to one another's tributes – we had been witness to one another's journeys and seen relationships revitalised and rejuvenated in our midst. The sum was much greater than our individual parts. Repeated experience of these "now moments" leads then to "moving along" together at a new and more attuned level (Stern, 2004). (See figure 3.6).

The second intervention that I want to recommend is the Circle of Security (CoS) (Powell et al., 2016), an approach which might be used in particular to support carers who perhaps have insecure attachment patterns from their childhoods thus are dismissing or preoccupied in their way of being with the person they are looking after. We understand that this can exacerbate an already difficult situation, as described above.

Central to this intervention programme is the CoS map (see Figures 4.4 and 4.5) which helps parents to discover, interpret, understand and respond to children's needs when they may find their behaviour challenging and their cues for attention mysterious. In a similar way to parents, caregivers of those who have dementia have to navigate a complex relationship where the emotional messages can be misunderstood and confusing (Powell et al., 2016).

This CoS intervention also uses video feedback to help caregivers see both what works well and where there is misattunement in their caregiving relationship. Frequently the caregiver's own history will be one where they have not had their emotional needs met so have a variety of insecure states of mind which can

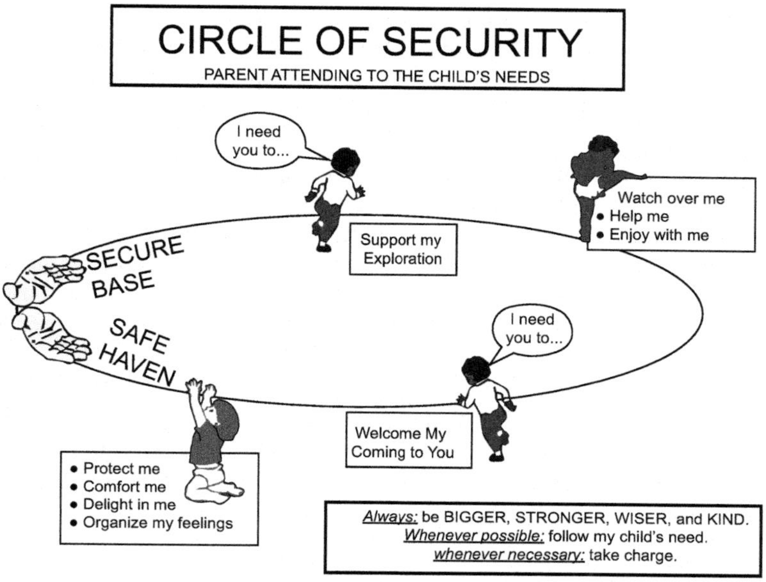

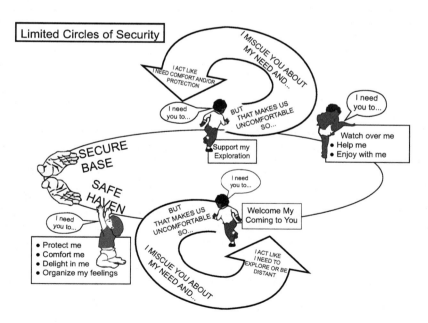

Figure 4.4 Circle of security

© 1998 Cooper, Hoffman, Marvin and Powell. Circleofsecurity.org

Figure 4.5 Limited circles of security

© 1998 Cooper, Hoffman, Marvin and Powell

be painful when put in situations where you are providing care and attunement to the very person who perhaps didn't help you to feel safe and attuned to as a child. The aim of this CoS group would be to support the carer in feeling heard and attuned to by other carers and professionals leading the group so as to enable them to both mourn the loss of what they never had and to hopefully reconfigure their internal working models of attachment through the attachment relationships they are developing with people in the project.

This is of course all hypothetical as no programme of this kind, as far as I am aware, exists but perhaps here is an opportunity to develop something new and effective as the fundamental learning from this project as has been demonstrated can be easily recognised and understood by participants from many different class and cultural backgrounds.

I now want to say a little more about how, in amongst all the complexity of the attachment dynamics of caregiver and care seeker, the fear system may intrude into any of the above, as well as emphasising that *all* these relationships take place in a social environment and a context of inequalities and external power dynamics (see Figure 4.2).

Person with dementia, family carer and professional carer

In this triad are the intersecting systems of:

* Attachment with reciprocal caregiving/care seeking
* Exploration
* Interest sharing
* Sexual and affiliative systems

(Heard et al., 2009)

We may have many examples of our own where fear has flooded a complex network of relationships where for example professional caregivers have become frozen in fear by what may feel like an overwhelming demand from a family in crisis and be unable to assess the escalating needs arising from a person's illness. The worker cannot think and plan clearly in her own context of fear arising from diminishing resources in the community and rising demands for overstretched services. Family and professionals may start to scapegoat each other as blame for the painful problems are left unaddressed or inadequately met. All this a microcosm of the intrafamily fears of the caregiver flooded by fear at the escalation of the disease process in their loved one.

What brings about change?

Finally, I want to address the big question – what do we know about the processes of change?

Of course, there is the wider issue of change at a societal level through political activism, which Angela Cotter's introduction has discussed. On an individual and dyadic level, I have found Dan Siegel's (2007) model for therapeutic change very hopeful and easy to grasp.

It is summarised in his COAL acronym – caregivers need to have:

• Curiosity
• Openness
• Acceptance and
• Love

Much of what we know is derived from parent infant research and micro observation. What we are looking for relationally in our support of those living with dementia is the equivalent of "something more than interpretation" from Daniel Stern's (1998) study group (see Figure 4.6).

They identified the following were key to experiences of therapeutic/relational engagement and change:

• Intersubjective moments of mutual recognition occurring between cared for person and caregivers which can create new internal organisation that can reorganise not only the relationship between them but the individual's implicit relational knowledge
• Implicit and non-verbal is the level at which communication of emotion is occurring
• Now moments and moments of meeting
• Moves to a new level of relating occur following now moments and moments of meeting

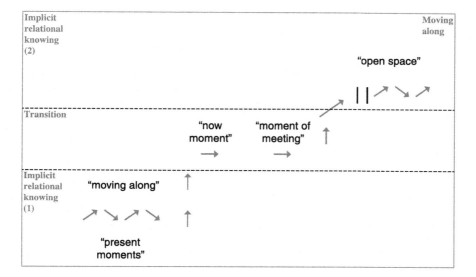

Figure 4.6 Creative cycles of change: micro-process of therapeutic change
Stern and colleagues, (1998)

- Visible in bodily changes – vitality affects – these bodily level changes indicate profound and visceral impact
- Changes in her or his way of being with others become evident following now moments and moments of meeting

However advanced the person's dementia may be, David Sheard (2013) posits that it is the communication of emotion that remains not mediated through language – but communicated body to body.

The second relational process I want to highlight with respect to promoting change is from the work of John Bowlby and his focus on the necessity for mourning loss when attachment relationships go through changes. This is very relevant for those living with dementia and their caregivers where patterns of relating are changed because of ageing, illness and disability.

Process of mourning

Bowlby, in collaboration with Colin Murray Parkes (2010), worked out the process of mourning but stressed that it is much messier than this diagram (figure 4.7) suggests. It is not smooth and linear as implied in the diagram.

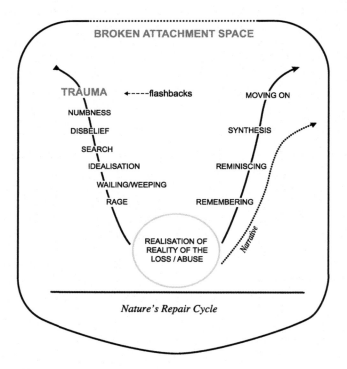

Figure 4.7 Process of mourning

© The Bowlby Centre, John Southgate and Andrew Odgers, 1998.

There are profound losses to mourn and many families who live alongside someone with dementia describe the mourning they go through together. See, for example, Hazel's moving account of supporting her sister "disappearing" in this volume. It is Bowlby's contention that by supporting people through a grieving process there is both gradual benefit and gradual recovery. With dementia the losses are painfully present as the person changes through their illness before their actual death. This faces us all with the impact of the changes in memory we all fear individually and collectively.

Finally, I want to bring to your attention the concept of "earned" security and how this might help us with a further way to understand both ourselves and those we may be caring for.

Earned security

Siegel outlines his theory regarding a fifth pattern of attachment behaviour: "earned secure attachment" (Siegel, 2007, p. 130). Such secure attachment can come through the experience of positive relationship in the wake of early trauma. The relationship is built through the attunement with the self that can occur through mindfulness, and also through interpersonal attunement that occurs through a positive attachment relationship – for example in therapy. Through this process he states:

> We bring curiosity, openness, acceptance and love to our own mind. In doing so we become our own best friends. Then we can develop a secure attachment to ourselves and heal some of the wounds we carry from having had parents who could not attune to us . . . Attunement might lead to the healthy growth of . . . the integrative and regulatory circuits of the brain.
>
> (Siegel, 2007, pp. 154–155)

Neuroplasticity, or brain plasticity, refers to the brain's ability to change throughout life. The human brain has the amazing ability to reorganise itself by forming new connections between neurons, thus new neural pathways can be developed through the experience of creative and healing relationships. I cannot emphasise enough the importance of new and stimulating creative activities affording the possibility of new relationships and adding to the quality of life of both the person with dementia and their carer(s). There is a comprehensive review of such provision in which the impact of community-based arts and health interventions on cognition in people with dementia is evaluated by Younga et al. (2016).

Scrapbooks expand personal story

One such intervention provided one of the remarkable "tools" my partner John and I learned to use together in the RYCT group – this was the use of a scrapbook to develop and share our memories.

This was both a very immediate and positive process of storytelling accompanied by finding photographs, drawing pictures to illustrate the stories and pasting these into large books. These books are now used when John goes to his different activities as a bridge to conversations with new people. So, this might be with family members at a mealtime or at the day centre or introducing him to a new caregiver. The message is: "This is part of the story of who I am and what I enjoy! We can talk about it together."

As Siegel points out, the valuable work of therapeutic healing takes place in right brain to right brain connection. There are parts of ourselves that we do not know – implicit, rather than explicit memories – as Schore summarised in an interview with Daniella Sieff:

> It takes painstaking, relational, embodied, long term psychotherapy (to heal early relational trauma). Emotional regulation, attachment patterns and dissociative defences are mediated by the right brain, so healing requires the kind of therapy that can work with the right brain. Because what is held by the right brain is not immediately available to consciousness, and because that which is dissociated is doubly difficult to access, it is a slow process.
>
> (Sieff, 2015, p. 128)

These principles can be equally applied to our community's relationship with those living with dementia as the emphasis is on the centrality of implicit relational interactions (right brain to right brain) in all our encounters best supported through establishing and maintaining long-term attachment relationships.

In conclusion I would like to add a personal reflection from my experience of being in a close and intimate relationship with someone who has Alzheimer's (being aware that each person's experience of this is uniquely different). I was thinking about the way in which Alzheimer's has obviously led to many losses in our lives together – losses of the way we used to discuss our work, play our music, travel and share our thoughts about the world and develop new ideas. This is sad and is mourned in an ongoing way, more clearly on some days than others.

As I was recognising the poignancy of these changes it was pointed out to me that in some other ways there are new patterns evolving of being together reflecting changes in John's identity and my own. John has always identified primarily as a jazz pianist – his great passion is be-bop in particular as well as loving the fusion he co-created with Indian classical musicians reflected in his innovatory group *Jazzindo*. He would never go to classical music concerts or art galleries with me – that was my thing! Not his! Since developing Alzheimer's it's as if there has been a "dyadic expansion in our senses of self". By this I mean he is now entranced by classical music of all kinds including chamber music, especially if it's performed live. He enjoys it even more if he is free to bring his own unique idiomatic bodily response to it namely whistling or providing an addition to the rhythm section. The welcome and encouragement from three groundbreaking projects *Music for the Moment, Music for Life* and *Songhaven,* led by professional musicians, are spaces where people living with dementia and their carers come together, to connect and communicate with each other in the here and now through music. They provide concerts that are inclusive and welcoming and opportunities to *play* using participatory musical improvisation (see note 2).

John also loves particular kinds of art, for example visiting David Hockney's exhibitions several times. These are novel activities for him in the last ten years. For my part my identity has expanded into community-based activism championing the cause of carers and to applying attachment theory principles to the needs of both carers and those they look after, especially those with dementia. It is our experience that it is possible to "live well together and remain intimately attached" in the context of John's illness provided there is sufficient support and resources to nourish our attachment relationship, enabling us to participate in a lively and meaningful way in our family and in the community. Our thanks go to all who make this possible both at home and in the community.

Notes

1   The perception of vitality forms is defined as "the felt experience of force in movement with a temporal contour and a sense of aliveness, of going somewhere" (Stern, 2010). Regardless of its content (thoughts, actions, emotions), the perceived Gestalt of vitality concerns the specific manner with which dynamic happenings unfold in space and time. It can thus be applied to every dynamic features emerging from the inter-personal relationships or time-based art expressions that "move us by the expression of vitality that resonate in us" (Stern, 2010, pp. 3–17).

2   **Music for the Moment** came about through a shared desire by the Royal Academy of Music, St Marylebone Parish Church and Resonate (Westminster Arts) to provide a concert series that was inclusive of people living with dementias. The partnership draws on the strengths and expertise of each organisation. The church provides a welcoming venue, Resonate provides grass-roots contact and support for people living with dementias, and students of the Royal Academy of Music perform. The project is mutually beneficial for all involved, with an opportunity for those living with dementias to participate and contribute, and students having an opportunity to experience their work in a broader context.

   Music for Life brings together professional musicians, care staff and people living with dementia through interactive music sessions. It aims to enhance the quality of life of its participants and to demonstrate to carers the emotional, social and physical potential of people in their care. Projects take place in residential homes and special day-care centres, and focus on people who can be isolated and disempowered as a result of the advanced stage of their dementia.

   During projects, specially trained musicians work alongside small groups of people with dementia and their carers, drawing out individuals and enhancing communication. These musical and personal interactions identify and build upon areas still intact in a person suffering the losses associated with the later stages of Alzheimer's and other forms of dementia – memory, physical capacities, personality changes and accompanying loss of identity.

   For further information see www.wigmore-hall.org.uk/learning/music-for-life (accessed 15 December 2017).

Songhaven is a professional concert series in central London that welcomes people living with dementia as well as their carers and companions. Hosted by mezzo-soprano Vivien Conacher, each Songhaven concert features special guest musicians, who perform an engaging programme together. Repertoire includes famous operatic arias, well-loved musical theatre tunes, and popular songs from the past. Everyone is free to be themselves at a Songhaven concert, which provides a warm and relaxed atmosphere. Audiences are encouraged to respond to the music as they choose – whether this be closing their eyes, moving to the beat, singing along, or even dancing. Noises and movement are not viewed as disruptions. Every concert finishes on a sing-along item, where audience members can join in with the professional singers to perform a well-known song together – always an uplifting experience for audiences and performers alike!

A post-concert afternoon tea then provides a wonderful opportunity for performers and audience members to mingle and chat about their favourite music. For further information see http://songhaven.co.uk/home/ (accessed 15 December 2017).

References

Ainsworth, M., Blehar, M., Waters, E., and Wall, S. (1978) *Patterns of Attachment: A Psychological Study of the Strange Situation.* Hillsdale, NJ: Lawrence Erlbaum Associates.

Alzheimer's Society (2017). www.alzheimers.org.uk/info/20027/news_and_media/541/facts_for_the_media. Accessed 22 November 2017.

Balfour, A. (2015). Living Together with Dementia: A Relationship Intervention for Couples Living with Dementia https://tavistockrelationships.org/images/TCCR_summary_of_the_LTwD_approach_Nov_2015_-_FINAL.pdf Accessed 5th June 2018.

Bowlby, J. (1973). *Attachment and Loss, Vol. 2: Separation Anxiety and Anger.* London: Tavistock.

Bowlby, J. (1980). *Attachment and Loss, Vol. 3: Loss, Sadness and Depression.* London: Tavistock.

Bowlby, J. (1988). The Origins of Attachment Theory. In: *Secure Base: Clinical Applications of Attachment Theory,* pp. 32–42. London: Routledge.

Carers Trust. (2017). https://carers.org/key-facts-about-carers-and-people-they-care for. Accessed 22 November 2017.

Clare, L., & Woods, R. T. (Eds) (2001). *Cognitive Rehabilitation in Dementia.* Hove: Psychology Press.

Feil, N. (2002). *Gladys Wilson and Naomi Feil.* YouTube clip. www.youtube.com/watch?v=CrZXz10FcVM. Accessed 15 December 2017.

Heard, D., Lake, B., & McCluskey, U. (2009, 2012). *Attachment Therapy with Adolescents and Adults: Theory and Practice Post-Bowlby.* London: Karnac.

Jones, G. M. M. (2011). Re-surfacing traumas not leaving people alone with fears and tears *Thoughts About Dementia* (TAD) Newsletter #36: 4 July.

Jones, G. M. M., van der Eerden-Rebel, W., & Harding, J. (2006a). Visuoperceptual-cognitive deficits in Alzheimer's disease: adapting a dementia unit. In: B. M. L. Miesen & G. M. M. Jones, (Eds). *Care-giving in Dementia, Vol. 4.,* pp. 3–58. London: Routledge.

Jones, G. M. M., Harding, J., van der Eerden-Rebel, W. (2006b). Visual phenomena in Alzheimer's disease: distinguishing between hallucinations, illusions, misperceptions and misidentifications. In: B. M. L. Miesen & G. M. M. Jones, (Eds). *Care-giving in Dementia,* pp. 59–104. London: Routledge.

Kitwood, T. (1997a). *Dementia Reconsidered.* Buckingham: Open University Press.

Kitwood, T. (1997b). The concept of personhood and its relevance for a new culture of dementia care. In: B. M. L. Miesen & G. M. M. Jones (Eds), *Care-giving in Dementia: Research and Applications, Vol 2*, pp. 3–13. London: Routledge.

Knocker, S. (2015). *Loving: The Essence of Being A Butterfly in Dementia Care.* London: Hawker Publications.

Knocker, S. (2018). Volunteering in Care Homes: Making Connections, Improving Lives. A short video. www.dementiacarematters.com/sally_knocker.html Accessed 1 June 2018.

Hesse, E., & Main, M. (2000). Disorganized infant, child, and adult attachment: Collapse in behavioral and attentional strategies. *Journal of the American Psychoanalytic Association, 48:* 1097–1127.

Miesen, B. M. L. (1999). *Dementia in Close-up: Understanding and Caring for People with Dementia.* London: Routledge.

Miesen, B. M. L. (2002). The Alzheimer Cafe. In: G. M. M. Jones & B. M. L. Miesen (Eds), *Care-giving in Dementia. Research and Applications, Vol 3*, pp. 307–333. Hove: Routledge.

Miesen B. M. L., & Jones, G. M. M. (1995). Psychic pain re-surfacing in dementia: from new to past trauma? In: C. Rowlings (Ed.), *Past Trauma in Late Life: European Perspectives on Therapeutic Work with Older People*, pp. 142–154. London: Jessica Kingsley.

Parkes, C. M. (2010) *Bereavement: Studies of Grief in Adult Life* (4th edition with Holly Prigerson, Ed.). London: Penguin.

Perren, S., Schmid, R., Herrmann, D., & Wettstein, A. (2007). The impact of attachment on dementia-related problem behavior and spousal caregivers' well-being. *Attachment & Human Development, 9*: 163–178.

Powell, B., Cooper, G., Hoffman, K., & Marvin, B. (2016). *The Circle of Security Intervention Enhancing Attachment in Early Parent-Child Relationships.* New York: Guildford.

Reifler, B. V., & Larson, E. (1990). Excess disability in dementia of the Alzheimer's type. In: E. Light & B. D. Lebowitz (Eds), *Alzheimer's Disease Treatment and Family Stress,* pp. 363–382. New York: Hemisphere.

Rich, A. (2013). *The Dream of a Common Language: Poems 1974–1977. Twenty-One Love Poems: Number X.* 1977. New York: Norton.

Robertson, J., & Robertson, J. (1989). *Separation and the Very Young.* London: Free Association Books.

Sabat, S. (2001). *The Experience of Alzheimer's Disease.* Oxford: Blackwell.

Schore, A. (2000). Attachment and the regulation of the right brain. *Attachment and Human Development, 2:* 23–47.

Sheard, D. (2012). *Feelings Matter* Most: *An Introduction* – Dementia Care Matters. Video. www.youtube.com/watch?v=YOUDrDGDZrE Accessed 1 June 2018.

Sheard, D. (2013). The feeling of mattering: The positioning of emotions in dementia care. *The Journal of Dementia Care, 21*(2): 23–27.

Sheard, D. (2018). *Our Dementia Care Philosophy.* www.dementiacarematters.com/our_dementia_care_philosophy.html Accessed 1 June 2018.

Schweitzer, P., & Bruce, E. (2008). *Remembering Yesterday, Caring Today – Reminiscence in Dementia Care: A Guide to Good Practice.* London: Jessica Kingsley.

Sieff, D. F. (2015). *Understanding and Healing Emotional Trauma: Conversations with Pioneering Clinicians and Researchers.* London: Routledge.

Siegel, D. (2007). *The Mindful Brain: Reflection and Attunement in the Cultivation of Well-Being.* New York: Norton.

Slade, A. (2008). *The Place of Fear in Attachment Theory and Psychoanalysis,* Annual John Bowlby Memorial Lecture, London.

Southgate, J. & Odgers, A. (1995). *Process of mourning – nature's repair cycle.* The Bowlby Centre (Centre for Attachment-based Psychoanalytic Psychotherapy) training course handout.

Steele, H., Phibbs, E., & Woods, R. T. (2004). Coherence of mind in daughter caregivers of mothers with dementia: Links with their mothers' joy and relatedness on reunion in a strange situation. *Attachment & Human Development, 6*(4): 439–450.

Stern, D. (2004). *The Present Moment in Psychotherapy and Everyday Life.* New York: Norton.

Stern, D. (2010). *Forms of Vitality: Exploring Dynamic Experience in Psychology, the Arts, Psychotherapy, and Development.* Oxford: Oxford University Press.

Younga, R., Camic, P., & Tischlerb, V. (2016). The impact of community-based arts and health interventions on cognition in people with dementia: a systematic literature review. *Aging & Mental Health,* 20(4): 337–351.

Chapter 5

Contemporary understanding of the aetiology, diagnosis and treatment approaches in relation to dementia

Susie M. D. Henley

In this chapter I will begin by explaining my setting and working role. I will then outline some statistics about memory, ageing, and dementia, before talking about how dementia is diagnosed in the clinic in which I work, treatment options, issues about help-seeking and diagnosis, and finish with some thoughts about what we could still do better.

My setting

I am a Clinical Psychologist specialising in working with people with long-term conditions such as dementia. Formerly I was attached to the "Specialist Cognitive Disorders" Clinic at the National Hospital for Neurology and Neurosurgery in London (www.uclh.nhs.uk/OurServices/ServiceA-Z/Neuro/CDC/Pages/Home. aspx). The clinic is a tertiary referral clinic, meaning that because it is specialist, it can accept referrals from all over the country as well as those in the local area. The team is led by Consultant Neurologists, and includes specialist nurses and neuropsychologists, visiting psychiatrists, and me. The focus of the clinic is on diagnosis of cognitive disorders, particularly dementia, and particularly rare, inherited, and young-onset (pre-65) dementias, as well as what are thought of as more "typical" older adult dementias where memory loss is usually a key feature. Patients and their families are offered follow-up, usually every six months to one year, and can access medical, psychiatric, and psychological treatments, but long-term and later-stage follow-up is often done by local community teams, closer to the patient's home.

Ageing and dementia

Some memory loss and other cognitive change is normal as people age (e.g., Rönnlund et al., 2005). It may have little impact on day-to-day life, or it may be due to treatable causes (e.g., Obstructive Sleep Apnoea, seizures or depression, all of which can have reversible effects on brain function) and improve after the appropriate intervention. Dementia is an umbrella term for a *progressive, neurodegenerative process*, that is, a pathological process in which brain cells progressively die, leading to increasing cognitive, behavioural and/or motor difficulties, which are irreversible.

At the time of writing there are estimated to be over eleven million people in the UK aged 65 and over (Annual Mid-Year Population Estimates for the UK, Office for National Statistics, 2015), which is about 17 percent of the population. Current figures suggest that there are over 700,000 people aged 65 or over with dementia, as well as 42,000 with dementia who are under 65 (Alzheimer's Society, 2014). For all of these people, Alzheimer's Disease (AD) is the most common cause of their dementia (accounting for around 62 percent), followed by vascular dementia (17 percent), mixed dementia (10 percent), Lewy Body Dementia (4 percent), Fronto-temporal dementia (FTD, 2 percent), Parkinson's dementia (2 percent), and other rare dementias (3 percent) (Alzheimer's Society, 2014).

The dementias typically differ in terms of their *pathology* (the underlying process that is causing neuronal death) and the *brain region(s)* affected. AD is caused by a specific pathology that usually (although not always) targets brain regions critical for memory (often the hippocampus on both sides of the brain). In the Fronto-temporal dementias a different pathological process affects the frontal and/or temporal lobes of the brain disproportionately, and as these regions, broadly speaking, underlie skills such as empathy, social interaction, planning and language, it is these skills that are primarily and most severely affected in this form of dementia; early signs of FTD might therefore be inappropriate behaviour, lack of empathy or difficulty with various aspects of speech and language, rather than memory problems. In Posterior Cortical Atrophy (PCA), a rare form of Alzheimer's disease, the pathology is found in the posterior parts of the brain, which are responsible for visuo-spatial skills. Early difficulties in PCA are often problems with walking upstairs, driving in poor light or reading, for example, whilst memory remains relatively intact. As alluded to above, a small but significant proportion of dementias are found in those under sixty-five, often people in their forties or fifties, and in very rare cases of AD and FTD there are known genetic causes for the dementia. The genes that cause "Familial" AD and FTD are autosomal dominant, meaning that a child of a parent with one of these types of dementia has a fifty percent chance of inheriting the gene that will inevitably cause dementia in them. These dementias are also usually of young-onset (i.e., onset in the 40s).

As the focus of the conference was on ageing and memory, the remainder of my chapter focuses on the most common form of dementia, "typical" AD, which is not inherited, tends to affect those over 65, and most frequently has memory problems as a defining feature. However, it is noteworthy that not all dementias are linked to ageing, or indeed involve memory loss, and interested readers are encouraged to use the Alzheimer's Society website (www.alzheimers.org.uk) and the University College London Rare Dementia Support Group websites (www.raredementiasupport.org) to access further information about these other forms of dementia.

Alzheimer's Disease

AD is the most common form of dementia, and typically the regions of the brain critical for memory (the hippocampus or the medial temporal lobe) are affected first. People with typical AD may show progressive difficulty with recalling events and people's names; they may become disoriented or lost, and repeat questions. Eventually, as the pathology spreads to other brain regions, they are likely to develop other cognitive problems. It is known that the risk of developing AD increases with age, that a healthy lifestyle and certain dietary factors may reduce this risk (e.g., Solfrizzi et al., 2011), and that the presence or absence of certain genes can also influence this risk (this is particularly well-explained on the Alzheimer's Society website www. alzheimers.org.uk/site/scripts/documents_info.php?documentID=168).   However, exactly why some people develop AD at some points, and others do not, is not clear.

To be diagnosed with Alzheimer's disease a number of criteria need to be met. Firstly, the broad criteria for any dementia must be met: symptoms must interfere with functioning, represent a decline from a previous level, not be attributable to a psychiatric disorder, and there should be evidence of cognitive impairment (in some domain) obtained both by taking a clinical history from the patient and someone who knows them well, and by objective testing (McKhann et al., 2011). Secondly, to meet criteria for "probable AD" further criteria must be met: the onset must be gradual (as opposed to sudden), with evidence that cognition is getting worse, and the most prominent cognitive deficits must be in one of four domains: memory (the most common), language, visuo-spatial, or judgement and problem-solving (McKhann et al., 2011). Again it is notable that memory is not the only, or indeed the most prominent feature of some presentations of AD. The pathology that underlies AD most frequently affects the memory areas of the brain, but can also affect the language, visuo-spatial or frontal areas preferentially, giving rise to "language", "visual" or "frontal" variants of AD.

Diagnosing Alzheimer's Disease

Reflecting on the criteria above, as well as the many different types of dementia, suggests that diagnosing AD is neither a quick nor simple process. Typically someone, possibly the patient, a partner or family member, notices that something seems wrong, and will begin to seek help, usually from a GP in the first instance. The GP may well refer on to other specialities with more experience of dementia, for example, a gerontologist, old-age psychiatrist, or (particularly for young-onset dementias) a neurologist.

Diagnostic criteria require that a history of progressive, insidious cognitive decline is obtained from both the patient and an informant who knows the patient well, and that an objective measure of function is also carried out, such as neuropsychological testing. A brain scan (usually a magnetic resonance image, MRI) is often recommended, to show *in vivo* evidence of brain atrophy in certain regions and to help rule out other, non-degenerative causes of difficulty such as a tumour. In some specialist centres such as the National Hospital, a lumbar puncture may also be recommended. This is an invasive procedure in which cerebrospinal fluid (CSF) is extracted from the spinal cord, and the ratio of proteins in the CSF is measured. In AD, this protein ratio tends to be different from normal ageing, or dementia due to a different pathology, and this can help aid diagnosis if there is a question about what pathology is underlying the difficulties the patient is experiencing. The patient may also be asked to have blood tests, again to rule out other possible causes of cognitive decline, and in some cases, with consent, to test for the known genetic causes of familial AD.

A key issue to be aware of are that all these investigations take time. For AD (or any dementia) to be diagnosed we have to be certain that this is something progressive, and we have to rule out other, potentially treatable, causes of cognitive decline. As change might be quite subtle in some cases it might be necessary to repeat certain investigations, typically the neuropsychological tests and the brain MRI scan, with a gap of at least ten months in between, in order to measure change objectively. The investigations may involve seeing different health professionals at different times. Often the need to investigate over time and with different professionals is not obvious to the patient and family and this needs to be made clear to them from the outset.

Guidelines for dementia diagnosis and support

There are a number of national guidelines recommending best practice in the diagnosis of dementia, and post-diagnostic support. The National Dementia Strategy (Department of Health, 2009) sets out key aims that people with dementia should get early diagnosis, information, and increased support. Alongside this the National Institute for Health and Care Excellence (NICE) has recommendations for both patients and carers (Fairbairn, Gould & Kendall, 2006). At diagnosis patients should be asked if they would like to know their diagnosis, and with whom this should be shared. It is important to assess and manage coexisting conditions (e.g., depression). It is recommended that written information is provided about a wealth of issues ranging from signs and symptoms, to medico-legal issues. NICE also makes clear that carers' needs should be assessed by Social Services, and this includes assessing for "psychological distress" and "psychosocial impact". Carers should be offered education about dementia, peer-support groups, information about services and benefits, and information about respite. Carers should also be offered psychological therapy if necessary. Thus there is a clear focus across these guidelines and recommendations for early diagnosis, information sharing, and support (both social and psychological) for both the person with dementia and someone who cares for them.

Treatment

There is at present no cure for any type of dementia. Symptoms can be alleviated slightly in a number of ways, and material and pragmatic support can also help both the person with dementia and their family.

Medication

There is evidence that some medications can improve cognitive symptoms slightly (e.g., Birks & Harvey, 2006). As with all medications they do not work in all people all the time, and there can be side effects and contraindications. Some GP practices are happy to prescribe these, or the person with dementia may need to be seen and followed-up at a more specialist centre such as a memory clinic or the Specialist Cognitive Disorders Clinic at the National Hospital. Medications are also available to influence mood and behaviour, although these are not specific to dementia, and there is limited evidence about their efficacy and safety (see e.g., Ballard et al., 2006; Seitz et al., 2011). It is likely that the person with dementia will need help or supervision to take the medication correctly.

Allied health professionals

There are an increasing number of allied health professionals with specialist dementia knowledge who can help maintain skills and a good quality of life. These include, but are not limited to: specialist occupational therapists who can assist with making the home safe and navigable; specialist physiotherapists who can recommend exercises for physical function; specialist speech and language therapists who can assist with speech, language and later on with swallowing and eating; and Admiral Nurses, specialist nurses who offer community support to the carer of someone with dementia.

Psychiatry

Psychiatrists are often consulted to help with specific issues that can arise with a dementia diagnosis, in particular risk (e.g., someone expressing suicidal thoughts); extreme mood difficulties (e.g., depression or anxiety); behaviour that others find challenging; and hallucinations and delusions which can be features of many dementias, in particular Dementia with Lewy Bodies, and can be extremely distressing for both the person with dementia and those around him.

Psychology

There are a range of psychological interventions for both people with dementia and their carers and an increasing evidence base that this can improve mood and quality of life, and reduce burden. Cognitive Stimulation Therapy (CST), a relatively intensive, short-term group-based intervention, has been shown to improve cognition and quality of life in people with dementia (Spector et al., 2003). Psychoeducation – spending time to teach people with dementia and carers about the different dementias – can also be very helpful and has been shown to be cost-effective (Livingston et al., 2013; Romeo et al., 2013). There is increasing evidence that one-to-one and group therapy to alleviate low mood or anxiety (using a range of therapeutic approaches) can be effective in dementia (Orgeta et al., 2014). In my service at the National Hospital there is also a demand for couples and relationship work as well as work with the wider family (in particular with adult children with a parent with dementia) although there is as yet less evidence about how effective interventions are for these groups. The Tavistock Relationships Centre has just finished a trial in which an attachment-based intervention was given to couples where one person had a dementia diagnosis and it will be very interesting to see what the impact of this was on the couples. Anecdotally, initial feedback from many of the couples has been very positive.

Pragmatic support

There are many other services that may be able to provide a variety of support for the person with dementia, and their carers. Regretfully they are not always obvious to the person with dementia and their family, and can take time to apply for. Firstly both the person with dementia and their primary carer are eligible for a "needs assessment" by their local Social Services team, which should identify support and equipment needed, and local resources that could help. Whilst not everyone will be eligible for state support, that should not preclude their being assessed and being informed of local help that they may then choose to pay for. Social Services can also help where there is a risk, for example, if the person with dementia, their carer, or children are put in a vulnerable position because of the situation.

Financially there are several allowances, both means-tested and non-means-tested, for which people with dementia or their carers may be eligible. Attendance Allowance (for people aged sixty-five and over with a "physical or mental disability"), Personal Independence Payment (for people under sixty-five) and NHS Continuing Care (payment for health needs) are all examples of non-means-tested financial support that depend on the person's level of impairment and health needs. Carers may be eligible for Carer's Allowance if they look after someone for at least thirty-five hours a week and do not earn over a certain threshold. See www.gov.uk/browse/benefits/disability for more information on this.

As the person with dementia may need help managing their affairs, and may reach a point at which they can no longer understand issues well enough to make complex decisions, a "Lasting Power of Attorney" can be set up in which the person with dementia gives their consent for someone else to manage certain affairs on their behalf. See www.gov.uk/browse/births-deaths-marriages/lasting-power-attorney for more information on this.

There are, in addition, practical forms of support, for example, obtaining a "blue badge" to be able to access disabled parking spaces; obtaining a "radar" key for access to public disabled toilets when out; "telecare" and personal alarm systems and many different aids to make everyday living easier for the person with dementia, for example, simple pre-programmed mobile phones and talking watches.

Access to help and interventions

There are a number of services that can offer some or all of the above interventions, or should be well-placed to advise the person with dementia and their families of where to look for other help. Most people with find their GP a good first port of call. Many people with dementia will be routinely followed-up by a more specialist team as well, for example, a Memory Clinic (specialists in diagnosing and treating dementia), a Community Mental Health Team (a multi-disciplinary team with the skills to help with a range of mental health issues, including those that might impact on someone with dementia) or tertiary centres such as the National Hospital for Neurology and Neurosurgery. Other local specialist teams may also be called upon if necessary, for example, a Continence Team or Challenging Behaviour Team if those issues become difficult for the person with dementia. In addition, there are a variety of day care services and activities for both carer and the person with dementia which can be a lifeline.

The voluntary sector

It is very important not to overlook the voluntary sector in the provision of help and support to people with dementia as well. The Alzheimer's Society (www.alzheimers.org.uk) exists to help all types of dementia (despite its name) and has very useful factsheets, phone lines, coffee mornings, and other events, with branches all over the country. Age UK (www.ageuk.org.uk) is a charity focusing on the wellbeing of older people, and offers a wealth of advice and sometimes face-to-face counselling for carers and people with dementia. This is not an exhaustive list, and there are many other charities for carers (e.g., www.carers.org), people with dementia (e.g., www.dementiauk.org) and people with mental health needs (e.g., www.mind.org.uk), all of which can provide advice and support. There are also many patient- and carer-led support groups, often for local people or for people with specific diagnoses, which are invaluable in offering people with dementia and their families a chance to share difficulties and solutions and simply talk to someone who is in a similar situation to them.

"Real life"

The above reads as if there is an overwhelming amount of help and support for people with dementia. In practice peoples' experiences can be very different. Some families with dementia may not seek help at an early point, perhaps because they do not recognise the difficulties as being dementia, or they have different cultural beliefs about how to treat and manage dementia, or because of the stigma surrounding a diagnosis. Some GPs struggle to recognise dementia, particularly if it is a rarer presentation (for example, non-memory-based and in someone under the age of 65). There is a pressure on resources for local services, many of which may require certain criteria to be met before they can work with someone (particularly age, as many services are split around the age of 65) and they may struggle to meet the cost of prescribing dementia medication. A lot of services have waiting lists and most psychosocial interventions are short-term and time-limited, although patients frequently point out that the "recovery" model, which is used in many mental health services, does not seem appropriate for dementia work where decline is inevitable. In addition patients and families report that they sometimes are left with no support at all, or that there are so many professionals involved that communication between teams seems to be very difficult and the family is left not knowing who to call in an emergency. A recent report suggested that many families feel unsupported and that GPs are reluctant to diagnose dementia at an early stage because they do not think that the right health and social care services are in place to help (Siddique, 2015).

So why diagnose?

There has recently been some debate in the literature over the perceived pros and cons of early diagnosis, for example, Le Couteur et al. (2013); but see also the response from Henley and Shakespeare (2013). There is a stigma associated with the disease; professionals can be reluctant to diagnose something for which there is no cure; there is a belief that giving a diagnosis might increase the risk of suicide amongst patients (but see Purandare et al., 2009); and there is concern that blanket screening (as opposed to symptom-led diagnosis) would give rise to false positives, that is, diagnosing someone with dementia when they do not have it, which is problematic. However, without a diagnosis people with dementia and their families cannot access any of the medical, health and social support mentioned above, and in addition patients themselves report that the uncertainty of not knowing what is wrong is very difficult to live with and that diagnosis can in fact be a relief (Carpenter et al., 2008).

What can we do better?

Recent reports from people with dementia and their families all suggest that there needs to be more awareness, both of the many different types and presentations of dementia, and of the help and support available. It is my opinion, backed up by the evidence cited above, that early diagnosis and intervention is preferable to late diagnosis, and we should be aiming to develop services to do this better. There needs to be improved communication between the many different agencies that may be involved in diagnosing and treating someone with dementia, and a focus on long-term follow-up as the person's needs change, not just brief support around the time of diagnosis. Finally it is extremely important to address the needs of carers and families as well as the named patient.

Research

There is increasing research across all aspects of dementia. Much of this focuses on finding and measuring "biomarkers" of progression, for example, changes in cerebrospinal fluid, brain imaging or cognitive tests, with a view to moving to clinical trials of compounds that might slow down or stop the various different pathologies (see Andrieu et al., 2015 for a recent review of clinical trials in Alzheimer's Disease). However there is also an interest in documenting the psychosocial effects of dementia on both patient, carer and families, and from that, developing psychosocial interventions to improve quality of life (e.g., Jensen et al., 2015).

Summary

Dementia is an umbrella term for a set of progressive, neurodegenerative diseases that can affect various cognitive domains, from mid-life onwards. The most common form of dementia is non-inherited, late-onset Alzheimer's Disease, which typically affects memory before other cognitive domains and for which symptoms are usually noticed late in life. Other, rarer forms of dementia include the fronto-temporal dementias, Posterior Cortical Atrophy, Vascular Dementia, and Lewy Body Dementia, many of which may be of young onset (prior to age 65) and some of which are inherited in an autosomal dominant pattern. There are clear guidelines for diagnosing the different dementias, and for what help, support, and symptomatic treatment should be offered to both people with dementia and their families, although in practice such help is not always sought or provided. Lack of awareness in the public and professionals, as well as limited resources, remain barriers to good practice. There is an increasing drive to increase awareness, and to pursue research into both drugs that might cure dementia, as well as other interventions to improve symptoms and quality of life for people diagnosed with dementia, and their families.

References

Alzheimer's Society. (2014). Dementia 2014: Opportunity for Change. https://www.alzheimers.org.uk/downloads/download/1484/dementia_2014_opportunity_for_change. Accessed 16 January 2018.

Andrieu, S., Coley, N., Lovestone, S., Aisen, P. S., & Vellas, B. (2015). Prevention of sporadic Alzheimer's disease: lessons learned from clinical trials and future directions. *The Lancet Neurology, 4422*(15), 70–72. http://doi.org/10.1016/S1474-4422(15)00153-2

Balfour, A. (2015). Living Together with Dementia: A Relationship Intervention for Couples Living with Dementia https://tavistockrelationships.org/images/TCCR_summary_of_the_LTwD_approach_Nov_2015_-_FINAL.pdf Accessed 5th June 2018

Ballard, C. G., Waite, J., & Birks, J. (2006). Atypical antipsychotics for aggression and psychosis in Alzheimer's disease. *Cochrane Database of Systematic Reviews, 1*, DOI: 10.1002/14651858.CD003476.pub2

Birks J., Harvey R.J. (2006). Donepezil for dementia due to Alzheimer's disease. *Cochrane Database of Systematic Reviews, 1*. Art. No.: CD001190. DOI: 10.1002/14651858.CD001190.pub2.

Carpenter, B. D., Xiong, C., Porensky, E. K., Lee, M. M., Brown, P. J., Coats, M. Morris, J. C. (2008). Reaction to a dementia diagnosis in individuals with Alzheimer's disease and mild cognitive impairment. *Journal of the American Geriatrics Society, 56*(3), 405–412. http://doi.org/10.1111/j.1532-5415.2007.01600.x

Department of Health. (2009). Living Well with Dementia: A National Dementia Strategy, 2009. http://doi.org/291591b 1p 4k

Fairbairn, A., Gould, N., & Kendall, T. (2006). *Dementia: Supporting people with dementia and their carers in health and social care. NICE Clinical Guideline.* March, 1–56.

Henley, S. M. D., & Shakespeare, T. J. (2013). *Rapid Response to: Political drive to screen for pre-dementia: not evidence based and ignores the harms of diagnosis.* Retrieved from http://www.bmj.com/content/347/bmj.f5125/rr/673541

Jensen, M., Agbata, I. N., Canavan, M., & McCarthy, G. (2015). Effectiveness of educational interventions for informal caregivers of individuals with dementia residing in the community: systematic review and meta-analysis of randomised controlled trials. *International Journal of Geriatric Psychiatry, 30*(2), 130–143. http://doi.org/10.1002/gps.4208

Le Couteur, D. G., Doust, J., Creasey, H., Brayne, C., & Couteur, D. (2013). Political drive to screen for pre-dementia: not evidence based and ignores the harms of diagnosis. *British Medical Journal, 347* (September), 1–6. http://doi.org/10.1136/bmj.f5125

Livingston, G., Barber, J., Rapaport, P., Knapp, M., King, D., Livingston, D., . . . Cooper, C. (2013). Clinical effectiveness of a manual based coping strategy programme (START, STrAtegies for RelaTives) in promoting the mental health of carers of family members with dementia: pragmatic randomised controlled trial. *British Medical Journal, 6276* (October), 1–14. http://doi.org/10.1136/bmj.f6276

McKhann, G. M., Knopman, D. S., Chertkow, H., Hyman, B. T., Jack, C. R., Kawas, C. H., . . . Phelps, C. H. (2011). The diagnosis of dementia due to Alzheimer's disease: Recommendations from the National Institute on Aging-Alzheimer's Association workgroups on diagnostic guidelines for Alzheimer's disease. *Alzheimer's and Dementia, 7*(3), 263–269. http://doi.org/10.1016/j.jalz.2011.03.005

Orgeta, V., Qazi, A., Ae, S., & Orrell, M. (2014). Psychological treatments for depression and anxiety in dementia and mild cognitive impairment. *British Journal of Psychiatry, 207*, 293–298.

Purandare, N., Voshaar, R. C. O., Rodway, C., Bickley, H., Burns, A., & Kapur, N. (2009). Suicide in dementia: 9-year national clinical survey in England and Wales. *The British Journal of Psychiatry: The Journal of Mental Science, 194*(2), 175–180. http://doi.org/10.1192/bjp.bp.108.050500

Romeo, R., Schehl, B., Barber, J., Livingston, D., Mummery, C., & Walker, Z. (2013). Cost effectiveness of a manual based coping strategy programme in promoting the mental health of family carers of people with dementia (the START (STrAtegies for RelaTives) study): a pragmatic randomised controlled trial. *British Medical Journal, 6342* (October), 1–12. http://doi.org/10.1136/bmj.f6342

Rönnlund, M., Nyberg, L., Bäckman, L., & Nilsson, L.-G. (2005). Stability, growth, and decline in adult life span development of declarative memory: cross-sectional and longitudinal data from a population-based study. *Psychology and Aging, 20*(1), 3–18. http://doi.org/10.1037/0882-7974.20.1.3

Seitz, D. P., Adunuri, N., Gill, S. S., Gruneir, A., Herrmann, N., & Rochon, P. (2011). Antidepressants for agitation and psychosis in dementia (Cochrane Review). *Cochrane Database of Systematic Reviews* (2). http://doi.org/10.1002/14651858.CD008191.pub2.

Siddique, H. (2015). Dementia patients forced to rely on unpaid carers, poll says. Retrieved from http://www.theguardian.com/society/2015/jul/06/dementia-care-alzheimers-society-survey-health. Accessed 17 October 2017.

Solfrizzi, V., Panza, F., Frisardi, V., Seripa, D., Logroscino, G., Imbimbo, B. P., & Pilotto, A. (2011). Diet and Alzheimer's disease risk factors or prevention: the current evidence. *Expert Review of Neurotherapeutics, 11*(5), 677–708. http://doi.org/10.1586/ern.11.56

Spector, A., Thorgrimsen, L., Woods, B., Royan, L., Davies, S., Butterworth (deceased), M., & Orrell, M. (2003). Efficacy of an evidence-based cognitive stimulation therapy programme for people with dementia: Randomised controlled trial. *The British Journal of Psychiatry, 183*(3), 248–254. http://doi.org/10.1192/bjp.183.3.248

Chapter 6

Shadow of loss hypothesis

Could attachment be the missing link in dementia research?

Richard Bowlby

This paper focuses on the links between a diagnosis of dementia and an individual's attachment history. I hope that by applying attachment theory to a new hypothesis, both dementia and attachment will be seen in a new light. The challenge is that we have to re-examine and change our most cherished beliefs and, just like trying to change our internal working model of attachment, change is difficult.

My career was working in scientific photography in medical research institutes in England, and my passion is the design of racing cars – I am not a psychologist or a psychotherapist – and I'm certainly not a neuroscientist. As John Bowlby's son I was privileged to witness the development of attachment theory first hand. I had frequent discussions about the everyday implications of his research, which was made possible because my wife Xenia and I lived next door to him with our two children. We were a three-generation extended family.

Most of this paper is based on factual information combined with well-established principles of attachment theory; however, I will also be presenting unproven hypotheses. As always, each of you must decide for yourselves whether there's anything that you want to take away with you. And always remember: an association between two factors does not prove that one causes the other.

Synopsis

In a privately researched pilot study of sixty people with dementia and sixty controls without dementia, the development of dementia in old age appeared to be associated with cumulative early loss in the maternal ancestral line. The findings were based on genealogical methods: family trees were created using only publicly available official records of births, marriages and deaths, and other official documents such as national censuses. This informal study was carried out by Jane Sherwood after she had retired from thirty-five years of social work in community and hospital settings in England.

The cumulative losses studied were passed on from grandmother, to mother, to baby – the baby being the person at increased risk of developing dementia in old age. In their earliest years, these babies were found more likely to have lost their father; or their mother may have lost another child or one of her own close siblings or her mother; and/or their maternal grandmother and/or great grandmother were likely to have had similar childhood losses. Attachment theory suggests that multiple intergenerational losses of loved ones could affect a mother's capacity to provide an adequate secure base during sensitive periods in the child's development. This experience could cast a shadow across the child's internal working model of attachment and their capacity for affect regulation (Liotti, 1992).

The "Shadow of Loss" hypothesis suggests that the combination of being raised in the shadow of loss and then encountering significant stress in mid to late life (e.g. the premature loss of loved ones) may lead to an increased dementia risk. The area of greatest conjecture is the assessment of risk that was made for each person in this informal pilot study, and the allocation of a score on a ten-point scale that was used to express the assessed risk. Developing a reliable assessment protocol and consistent scoring procedure will be the most challenging task for future research to test this hypothesis.

Without effective affect regulation from a sensitive attachment figure, distressing childhood experiences are unlikely to be adequately resolved, and memories of the distress may emerge in later life at times of reduced resilience or increased threat to attachment security. This raises the question of whether appropriate psychological therapies might in time have a role to play in the dementia field. Possible opportunities for therapy might focus on: people starting to struggle with cognitive impairment in later life; parents who have been bereaved during pregnancy or the early life of their baby and who have already lost someone close during their own childhood; and children, families and older individuals who are not managing to resolve their feelings following bereavement or other traumatic experiences. This hypothesis needs formal testing.

Key concepts from attachment theory and John Bowlby's life relevant to this research

In attachment theory (the science of love), John Bowlby gave us the internal working model of attachment, where both positive and negative events in childhood impact the subconscious expectation of the availability of care and affection. The ability of a child's primary attachment figure to provide a secure (or an insecure) attachment relationship will be affected by the parent's own positive and negative experiences of family life when they were growing up. The clinical psychologist Roy Muir (1994) put it this way, "People say parenting comes naturally, it does, but it comes naturally the way we *learned* it – it doesn't come naturally to do it *differently*". This is one of the key elements in the intergenerational transmission of attachment.

Allan Schore (1994) gave us affect regulation and the infant's experience-dependent maturation of the right hemisphere of the brain, where the interaction between a baby and its environment (especially with the primary attachment figure – usually the birth mother) will directly affect the neuronal density and synaptic connections that become established during the growth spurt of the right brain in the first year or two of life. Whereas food and shelter provide the *physiological* needs for the survival of a fragile baby, what's essential for their *psychological* maturation is having their *emotional* needs met. These early experiences can influence the child's capacity to regulate their affect in stress and in joy throughout their life. The theoretical concepts of Bowlby and Schore are central to this concept because they help us to *deduce* what attachment experience may have happened in the past that could *explain* present outcomes. And they help us to *predict* the outcome that attachment experiences in the *present* may produce in the *future*.

But first let me tell you a little bit about my father's background. John Bowlby was a medical doctor, a consultant child psychiatrist, an adult and child psychoanalyst and a psychologist. His first training was in Natural Sciences from Cambridge, so first and foremost he was a scientist. Melanie Klein was his training supervisor for child analysis. Two of the cornerstones of the science of attachment theory are Ainsworth's (Ainsworth et al., 1978) Strange Situation Procedure and Mary Main's Adult Attachment Interview, known as the AAI (George et al., 1996). The AAI asks about the interviewee's recollections of their early childhood relationship with their "primary attachment figure", and if there's any doubt about who should be considered the primary attachment figure in childhood, the question will be asked – "Who would you say raised you?" or "Who brought you up?" For me, it was my mother – my biological mother Ursula – who raised me. I was born in 1941 during the Second World War. To avoid the bombing in London, my mother had moved to the countryside of Southern England to stay with her own mother whilst my father was an army psychologist. Thus I was born in rural Wiltshire, in my grandmother's house and raised by my mother. But if you'd asked my father – John Bowlby – "Who raised you?" he would have said that his nanny raised him. In his parents' well-to-do London family there were six children. The two eldest girls, my aunts, were raised by the family nanny – Nannar. (I knew Nannar because she continued to live with my grandmother as her companion and housekeeper until my grandmother died aged 90 – when I was 16.)

Nannar was busy with the two eldest girls when my uncle Tony was born, so she was raising three young children. However only thirteen months after Tony was born, along came John. With four children to care for they decided more help was needed and they employed an under-nanny for John. She was called Minnie and was about 17 when she arrived. Minnie was a full time live-in nursemaid. My father told me that he became attached to Minnie, the "one person who steadily 'mothered' him" (Minnie has said that John was her favourite), but when John was 4 or 5 years old, Minnie left the Bowlbys to get a more senior job with another family. My father told me (Bowlby, personal communication, no date) that he remembered the pain of loss when Minnie left, and that he was "sufficiently hurt but not sufficiently damaged" to use this experience as a daily inspiration for his research.

But how does this work? I was born in my grandmother's house and raised by my mother, and my father was born in his mother's house and raised by Minnie.

What experiences led *me* to choose my mother, and my *father* to choose Minnie? By about six months most babies start to show a preference for one person over the other people in their life – especially noticeable when they're distressed. But what do babies experience during the first six months of life that leads them to show a preference for one particular person? They recognise the person who most frequently comforts them when distressed and reduces their negative affect, and who most frequently brings them joy, and increases their positive affect. But just because frequency of care is linked to the selection of a *primary* attachment figure, frequency is not closely linked to how *secure or insecure* the baby's attachment will be. *Sensitivity* and *attunement* are more closely linked to security of attachment. I believe that Minnie provided that primary attachment for John, and when she left he was heartbroken. I think the family script in the Bowlby household before the First World War would have been to dismiss the significance of his feelings for someone who was "only" an employee. My view is that John Bowlby would have been classified as "insecure avoidant" – he had very strong feelings but was inhibited about showing them. There's no doubt in my mind that losing Minnie was the start of my father's quest to make sense of his feelings.

Humans have the most astonishing brains, but the price we pay is that we have to make sense of our feelings. And when our feelings or experiences are dismissed or contradicted, as I think were my father's when Minnie left, we feel we are going mad. We're not going mad, we're just very confused – and staying confused for too long can drive us crazy – especially if we've buried the bad memories and shut away the feelings. In many ways I think the greatest value of attachment theory is to provide us with a way to understand the origins and nature of our most powerful feelings. Having this understanding gave my father the strength and determination to persevere with his work – even when faced with scepticism and hostility from many of his peers.

Attachment theory predicts that the quality of attachment that is developed during childhood will continue into later life – for better or worse. This is especially true if life circumstances remain unchanged. However, if a child experiences significant change in their attachment circumstances, then a significant change in the child's attachment classification can be expected – for better or worse. Factors that can *prevent* a child from developing a secure primary attachment to a parent will often have their origins in the parent's own childhood (usually that of the mother who has traditionally, in our society, been the primary caregiver) often in combination with present experiences.

For instance – what's the likely impact on a parent's capacity to provide sensitive and attuned care for a new baby, if their partner has recently died – or if one of their older children has recently died? How might the parent's grief and emotional unavailability impact upon the baby's emotional and neurobiological development? Grief and mourning after the loss of a loved-one is frequently overwhelming, at least in the short-term, and must rank amongst the most painful of all human experiences. The accumulation of multiple losses within a family may have an impact on child development that's greater than the sum of the parts – with each additional loss *compounding* the trauma of the previous one.

Unresolved loss is a particular problem that is associated with social and emotional family problems, and with varying degrees of psychopathology. It's usually the combination of several significant risk factors that increase the likelihood of being overwhelmed emotionally. However, although infant mortality and premature death of young parents are no longer common in the twenty-first century, premature deaths were much more common in the childhoods of those people who now have dementia, and even more common in their parents' and their grandparents' lifetimes.

Jane Sherwood's research

I'm going to describe the work of Jane Sherwood. Jane has been investigating the family histories of people who have developed Alzheimer's disease or other dementias in old age. Since 2012 I've been in regular discussion with Jane who has been developing a new research protocol using attachment theory to interpret the data. This highlights a potential risk factor in childhood which may be associated with dementia in old age.

In order to prevent a medical disease, first it's necessary to know what's causing it. For instance, how could an effective AIDS treatment have been developed, if it hadn't first been discovered that AIDS was caused by a virus? Equally, how can effective prevention or treatment for dementia be developed if we don't know what's causing it. On the website of the Alzheimer's Society it states, "The cause or causes of Alzheimer's disease are not yet known. However, most experts agree that Alzheimer's, like other common chronic diseases, develops as a result of multiple factors rather than a single cause." And also, "The greatest risk factor for Alzheimer's disease is advancing age, but Alzheimer's is not a normal part of ageing." (Alzheimer's Society, 2017)

Jane's informal study was started in 2010. In her privately funded and researched pilot study of sixty people with dementia and sixty controls without dementia, the development of dementia in old age appeared to be associated with cumulative early loss in the maternal ancestral line – those who developed dementia seemed to have been *"raised in the Shadow of Loss"*. Jane's research protocol and findings were based on genealogical methods to create family trees using *only* publicly available records of births, marriages and deaths, and official documents such as national censuses. No medical records were used. Jane Sherwood's study does not establish causality; it's unpublished and this data and any conclusions should be considered to be preliminary until replicated and published in a peer-reviewed journal.

Since 2012, Jane has focused on the ancestral history of two groups of people – sixty who had dementia, and another sixty people for comparison who did not have dementia by the time they died aged over 80. Jane noticed a pattern of cumulative early loss in the maternal line of the people who developed dementia which she *hypothesized* would have cast a shadow over their early development, and this might be associated with developing dementia in old age. Jane's genealogical technique requires *at least* three generations of ancestral records (preferably four generations) in the direct maternal line for every person in both of her study groups in order that she can draw-up an adequate family tree for each person. For somebody now aged over 80, three generations will date back to the middle of the 1800s. In those days, the mothers raised the children, and the fathers worked to provide for the family.

The cumulative losses of people in the d*ementia* group were passed on from *grandmother*, to *mother*, to *baby* – the *baby* being the person at increased risk of developing dementia in old age. These babies were found more likely to have lost their father in their earliest years; and/or their mother had suffered intimate loss in childhood and then in young adulthood had lost a child or one of her own close siblings or her mother; and/or their *maternal grandmother* and/or *great grand-mother* were likely to have suffered similar premature losses.

The work of Bowlby and Schore suggests that premature losses of loved-ones in a mother's life, and/or in her recent ancestral background, could compromise the secure base she would be able to provide for her child, especially if the losses happened during a sensitive period of the child's development. In Jane's findings, the age of the baby when her or his primary attachment figure encountered bereavement appears to be important. This might explain why one particular baby should develop dementia while her or his older and younger siblings escape.

A child's primary attachment figure will handle the loss of a loved one (spouse or partner, parent, adult sibling, baby or child) more or less successfully depending upon their own childhood experience of how *their* family dealt with painful feelings. Without effective affect regulation from a sensitive attachment figure, distressing childhood experiences are unlikely to be adequately resolved. The unresolved memories from childhood may become buried, only to re-emerge if attachment security is threatened, at times of reduced resilience, when ill, or in later life.

The death of a father during childhood has been found to triple the risk of developing dementia in late life (Tschanz et al., 2005) – although a child of a father who had never been present does not appear to be at increased risk of dementia (despite the material hardship and stigma associated with illegitimacy a century ago). In those days, most mothers of illegitimate children did not usually have a co-habiting life-partner, so the *absence* of a child's father would not have been experienced as *bereavement* by the mother.

In later life, additional risk factors for developing dementia include outliving a spouse or partner. In 2009 Håkansson reported that, "The highest increased risk for Alzheimer's disease was in carriers of the apolipoprotein E e4 allele *who lost their partner before mid-life and were still widowed or divorced at follow-up*" (Håkansson et al., 2009). And in 2014 Sundström and colleagues (Sundström et al., 2014) reported that, "Our findings suggest that marital and parental status are important risk factors for developing dementia, with especially increased risk in those being *both widowed and without children*."

The "Shadow of Loss" hypothesis suggests that the *combination* of being raised in the shadow of loss, *and then* encountering significant stress in mid to late life, may lead to an increased risk of dementia.

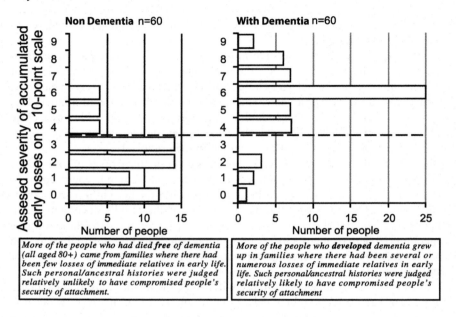

Figure 6.1 Cumulative childhood loss across three generations

Sherwood 2013. Provisional data only

Figure 6.1 shows the non-dementia comparison group on the left, and the dementia group on the right – the dashed horizontal line between three and four is to aid comparison only – the length of each bar represents a *percentage* of people in each group of sixty.

The *degree* of premature losses experienced by each participant are on the vertical axis – the greater the losses the higher the score. The number of participants experiencing a similar degree of losses is on the horizontal axis – the longer the bar, the more people with that degree of loss. Towards the bottom of the non-dementia chart, there are more people with fewer losses (20 percent had no premature losses at all for three generations and scored zero). And towards the top of the dementia group there are many people with more losses, 4 percent of the dementia group scored a maximum of nine. The assessment of perceived risk on a scale from zero to nine that Jane has made for each person in this informal pilot study is the area of greatest uncertainty, and calls out for research.

Jane Sherwood gave the following description to the background of her prototype scale:

It was suggested that I try using my social work knowledge and experience of the impact of broken attachments to apply a simple ten-point scale to the number and severity of the childhood losses in the maternal line of each of the 120 backgrounds of the people in my study. I was guided by the following parameters:

- Backgrounds where there had been no bereavements during the early life of the individual in my study, or of their mother, or of their maternal grandmother, scored zero (at the bottom of the scale).
- Backgrounds scored nine where the catalogue of childhood losses/ separations was so extreme that it was hard to imagine how any further tragedies could have made early life significantly worse (at the top).
- All the remaining backgrounds were ranked in relation to these two extreme scores and to each other.

Non-dementia group

Well established research findings recognise that the risk of developing dementia increases with age – especially over the age of 80. The combination of being over 80 and also outliving a partner therefore carries a significant degree of risk for developing dementia, yet there are many people in this situation who don't get dementia. In an attempt to reduce confirmation bias it was decided that these two risk factors – being over 80 and outliving a partner – should form part of the selection criteria for a comparison group of sixty people who were all free of dementia.

Through her genealogical and other contacts Jane recruited a random but not randomised **non-dementia** comparison group of sixty people who each fitted the following four selection criteria:

- they must all have been free of dementia when they died
- they must all have died over the age of 80
- they must all have outlived their partners, or been divorced or never married
- they must all have at least three generations of official records in the maternal line

Jane constructed a family tree for each of the 120 people in her study to examine their history of premature loss in the recent ancestral past of their maternal line. Figures 6.2 and 6.3 show two family trees, one from the **non-dementia** group and another from the group **with dementia**.

Ursula's family tree

Ursula was my mother, and she did *not have* dementia when she died from pneumonia aged 83 – ten years after my father had died from a stroke also aged 83 (and also free of dementia). Ursula met all four selection criteria for the non-dementia comparison group and has been included in it.

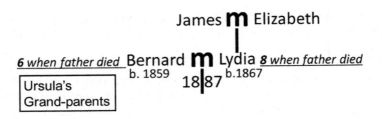

James **m** Elizabeth

6 when father died Bernard **m** Lydia *8 when father died*
b. 1859   18|87 b.1867

Ursula's
Grand-parents

Ursula (83)
1917-2000

Figure 6.2

Sherwood 2013

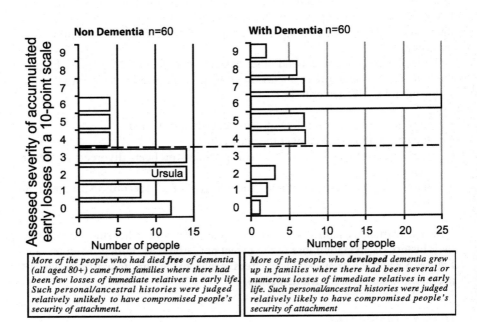

More of the people who had died *free* of dementia (all aged 80+) came from families where there had been few losses of immediate relatives in early life. Such personal/ancestral histories were judged relatively unlikely to have compromised people's security of attachment.	More of the people who **developed** dementia grew up in families where there had been several or numerous losses of immediate relatives in early life. Such personal/ancestral histories were judged relatively likely to have compromised people's security of attachment

Figure 6.3 Cumulative childhood loss across three generations

Sherwood 2013. Provisional data only

James and **Elizabeth** were Ursula's maternal *Great* Grandparents (four generations back). **Lydia** was an only child, (and was Ursula's maternal Grandmother) – **Lydia** lost her father **James** when she was eight, leaving her mother **Lydia** a grieving widow. **Lydia** married **Bernard**, who had also lost his father at six, and also leaving his mother a grieving widow. (Jane has noticed that several married couples had similar childhood losses.) However, **Lydia** and **Bernard** had made it through the first years of life before the loss of their fathers struck them and their widowed mothers.

Note: The death of a father is also the death of a husband, and this would cause his child(ren) and his widow to simultaneously grieve the loss of a significant attachment figure. The loss may have had a more detrimental effect on the children if it had happened when they were very young and at a time when they were developing their primary attachment to their mother. Her grief at that time could obstruct her ability to form a secure bond to her baby and to become a secure attachment figure. This is the sort of interpretation that Jane has made based on attachment theory.

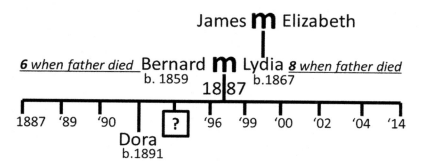

Figure 6.4
Sherwood 2013

Lydia and **Bernard** had four children in quick succession – then a gap of five years – and then five more children in quick succession, and then a late afterthought in 1914. The fourth child was **Dora** (who became Ursula's mother). The question is – did **Lydia** have a miscarriage or a still-birth when **Dora** was between 2 and 5 years old that had not been recorded? If there *had* been a loss – would **Lydia's** grief prevent her from providing **Dora** with sensitive care? Or was there a nanny? Or was **Dora** reasonably unaffected, but the next baby (**Bernard** b. 1896)

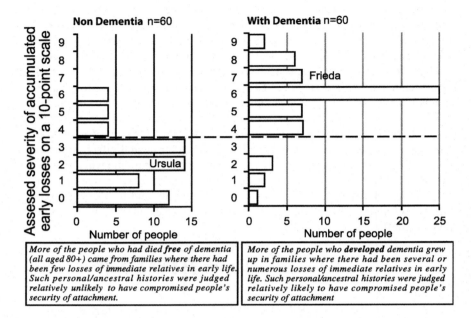

Figure 6.5 Cumulative childhood loss across three generations

Sherwood 2013. Provisional data only

significantly more affected? (O'Leary & Gaziano, 2011). These questions cannot be answered because there are no public records, but they will be taken into consideration by Jane in her assessment of Ursula's score.

Note. **Bernard** was **Dora's** favourite brother, but he was killed in action in France in 1916 during the First World War – only a year before Ursula was born.

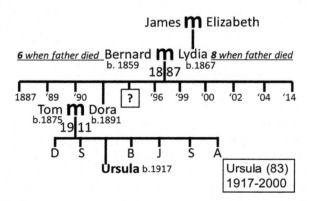

Figure 6.6

Sherwood 2013

Dora married **Tom** – and their third child **Ursula** was born in 1917 during the First World War when her father was serving in the Far East, (in Simla with the Gilgit Scouts). How would **Dora** have coped with no spousal support from **Tom** during Ursula's first few years? **Dora** also had her first two children to care for – both under 5 years old.

Ursula married **John Bowlby** in 1938. There was no dementia during these four generations in my mother's maternal ancestral line.

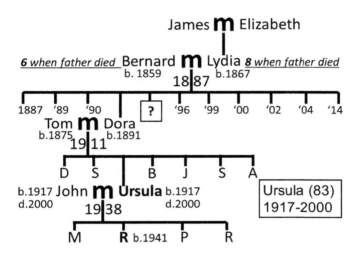

Figure 6.7
Sherwood 2013

To put the scale into perspective, Jane gave **Ursula** a score of two. **Ursula** had a few risk factors – but she did not develop dementia.

Dementia group

There's much discussion amongst professionals about the exact diagnosis of dementia. In this informal and self-funded project, Jane established the absence or existence of dementia as best she could – from direct personal knowledge, or from reliable informants and from death certificates. Jane did not discriminate between the different forms of dementia.

Note: Alzheimer's disease is the most common form of dementia.

The second example is from the **dementia** group. This was another random but not randomised group of sixty people all of whom were acknowledged to have (or have had) some form of advanced dementia in old age, had outlived their spouse, and for whom there were *at least* three generations of official records in the maternal line.

Frieda's family tree

Frieda was my wife Xenia's paternal grandmother, who died aged 88 with dementia. She met all the selection criteria and was included in the **dementia** group.

In 1854, **Isabella** (**Frieda's** grandmother) was 24 when she married **William**. **Isabella** was already pregnant, and her mother had died the previous year. Their first child **Laura** was born the same year – 1854.

Note: **Isabella** may have been vulnerable as a first-time mother. She had just lost her own mother, and her father had become a widower, she was already pregnant with **Laura** and not yet married – although she did marry before the baby was born. It is possible that **Laura's** foetal development may have been compromised by the elevated level of maternal stress – and **Laura** became **Frieda's** mother.

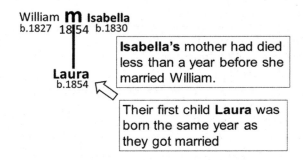

Figure 6.8

Sherwood 2013

Isabella had a second child in 1856. Meanwhile, in 1856/7, **Isabella's** father had died when baby **Laura** was only 2 or 3 years old. So, **Isabella** had lost both her parents by the time she was 26 or 27 and was almost certainly grieving whilst she was raising **Laura.**

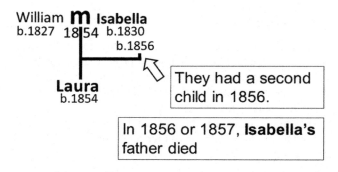

Figure 6.9

Sherwood 2013

Isabella and **William** had a third child in 1859. But in 1860, the third child died when only a year old and when **Laura** was 6.

Note: To what extent might **Laura's** development have been affected by her mother's loss of her parents plus the loss of a child; would this affect **Isabella's** ability to provide **Laura** with a secure attachment? **Laura** will have developed an internal model of how painful feelings are handled within the family. To what extent can painful feelings be expressed? And what degree of comfort might she expect from her (grieving) attachment figures?

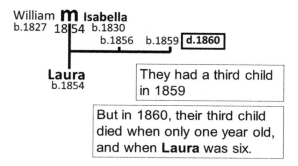

Figure 6.10

Sherwood 2013

When **Laura** (**Frieda's** mother) was 17, she married **David** and they had a son **Thomas** the following year.

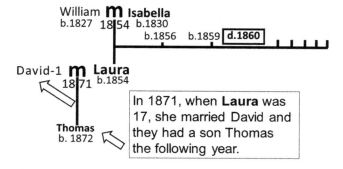

Figure 6.11

Sherwood 2013

However, when **Laura** was 23, her husband **David** died aged only 27 leaving **Laura** with 5-year-old **Thomas**. **Thomas** was later recorded in the national census as living with his grandmother **Isabella**.

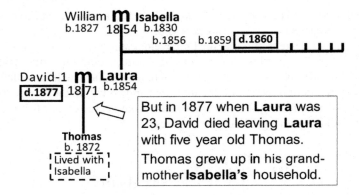

Figure 6.12

Sherwood 2013

Three years after **David** had died, **Laura**, aged 26, married **Augustus** and they had two children, **Paul** and **Frieda** – born eighteen months apart.

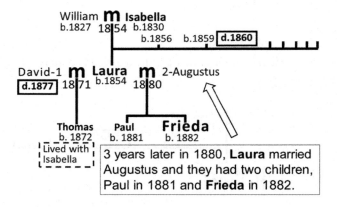

Figure 6.13

Sherwood 2013

One year after **Frieda** was born, **Augustus** died at the age of only 34. **Laura** was a widow for the second time at the age of 29 – **Frieda** was only a year old – a very sensitive period for her neurobiological and psychological development.

Note: I have all the official certificates as evidence for these events.

Jane Sherwood has this to say:

What are the options for someone in Laura's dreadful position? Laura might have done her utmost to cover up her sadness in front of her children. But children readily pick up the signals. They also learn how to handle their own emotions from what they witness their parents doing.

With the best will in the world, Laura is likely to have been less tolerant of the demanding, attachment-seeking behaviour of a toddler daughter than she would have been without a recent bereavement.

There were surely times when Laura couldn't help being distracted by her distress and worry, perhaps becoming rather unresponsive. It's all too easy for a young child in this situation to grow up sensing "My feelings and needs don't count". This experience deprives a child of growing up treating her/his **own** needs seriously, and being able to "self-soothe" in times of heightened emotion.

Addictions tend to be born out of such faulty early learning. Anyone in Laura's calamitous position would be at constant risk of breaking down in front of her children. What does that convey to a young child? Where has his/her security gone? We know that slightly older children actively fear abandonment when one parent has gone and the other appears vulnerable.

Note: It would seem that **Laura's** internal working model of loss during childhood was all too accurate. After losing two husbands could **Laura** then have provided one-year old **Frieda** with a secure attachment? I don't think so. **Laura** did not marry again. She was a single mother and became a milliner – a hat maker. I assume that **Laura** would have struggled financially to raise her two children **Paul** and **Frieda** – **Thomas** may have been living with his grandmother **Isabella** (according to the national census).

Frieda was the only daughter of a twice widowed single mother growing up in Victorian times without a father or welfare and I think **Frieda** would have been very vulnerable to social and emotional problems. From an attachment theory perspective, **Frieda** had a very difficult start in life during a sensitive period of development and I think this somehow holds the key to her increased vulnerability for developing dementia in her eighties.

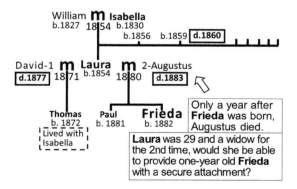

Figure 6.14
Sherwood 2013

When **Frieda** was 24 her half-brother **Thomas** died aged 34.

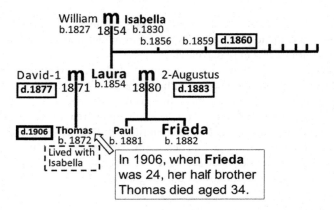

Figure 6.15

Sherwood 2013

One year after **Thomas** had died, and when **Laura** may still have been grieving his loss, **Frieda** married **Douglas** when she was 25 – they had two children. A son, **Roderick**, who became my father-in-law, and a daughter.

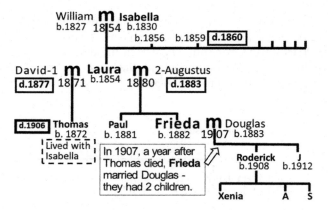

Figure 6.16

Sherwood 2013

Note: **Frieda** was very beautiful and married well. **Douglas** was a success-ful lawyer who became President of the Law Society and he was knighted – so **Frieda**'s title was Lady. They had a lovely house in the country and a house in London near Hampstead Heath.

When **Frieda** was 32 and **Roderick** was 2, **Frieda's** grandmother **Isabella** died aged 80, and five years later **Frieda's** mother **Laura** died aged 61 when **Frieda's** second child was only 3. **Frieda** therefore lost her grandmother and mother at a time when she was raising two small children. How free would **Frieda** have been to grieve the loss of her mother and grandmother? Would **Frieda** have buried these painful feelings leaving them as "unresolved losses"?

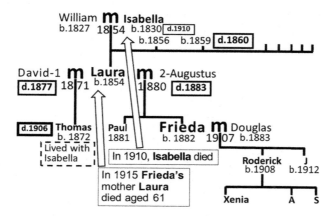

Figure 6.17
Sherwood 2013

Frieda's husband **Douglas** died aged 66 (when **Frieda** was 67). **Frieda** was left well off by **Douglas**, but outliving a partner is associated with an increased risk factor for developing dementia.

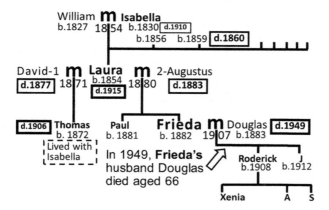

Figure 6.18
Sherwood 2013

When **Frieda** was 76, her older brother **Paul** died aged 77.

Note: I met **Frieda** several times; she lived nearby in Hampstead with her widowed daughter – **Frieda** felt the loss of her son-in-law very much. By about 1965 **Frieda** started to develop dementia and she went to live in a North London care home for the last few years of her life.

After living for twenty-one years as a widow, **Frieda** died aged 88 in 1970. **Frieda's** death certificate records the cause of death as I. Virus Pneumonia, and II. Senile Dementia.

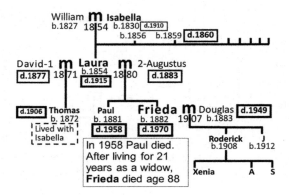

Figure 6.19

Sherwood 2013

Here is **Ursula's** family tree for comparison.

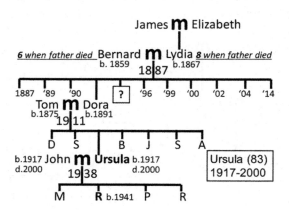

Figure 6.20

Sherwood 2013

To put the scale into perspective, Jane scored **Frieda** as seven.

Discussion

I found Ursula's and Frieda's family histories very moving. Luck plays such a large part in our lives today, but how much more precarious were the lives of our parents and grandparents. It strikes me that whilst Ursula's history and childhood was "secure enough", Frieda's history and her catalogue of losses throughout life would have created a pervading sense of vulnerability and fear that was not "secure enough". At sensitive times of her life Frieda would likely have felt helpless to fend for herself and hopeless that others would care for her; either because they were overwhelmed by grief themselves or because they were elsewhere – or had died. The consequences for Frieda of living in the shadow of loss were profound – yet no one was to blame.

Although Jane Sherwood's study used mainly official records of births marriages and deaths to establish the dates of possible traumatic losses, there will be other experiences that are traumatic – such as abuse and neglect – but there are no public records for these adverse childhood experiences that date back 150 years.

Attachment seeking behaviour

There are certain times in life, from cradle to grave, when we feel more vulnerable than normal and we have elevated needs to access our primary attachment figure. These include separations, getting lost, darkness, ill heath, pregnancy, new-parenthood, old age, and of course bereavement. These situations produce elevated levels of proximity seeking behaviours such as searching and calling-out for the loved-one; and if proximity is not achieved the anxiety increases and attachment seeking behaviour escalates. If children's attachment seeking remains unresponded to for several days, the child may become emotionally and socially withdrawn, and this can lead to psychological problems in later life.

The brain is an "historic organ" with new experiences that are layered on top of earlier ones. A new experience does not delete an older one, but a new neural network can develop in response to new experiences which can modify the mind's internal working model. Although the premature death of a loved-one will remain a significant event throughout life, it does not automatically lead to the bereaved person developing emotional problems. The outcome will depend partly on their own experiences and internal working model of attachment, and partly on the emotional availability and capacity for affect regulation of the bereaved person's attachment figure. This may prove difficult in practice because the attachment figure may also be grieving the loss of the same loved-one, and their emotional availability in this situation will depend on their own internal working model – much of which was developed during childhood with *their* parents. This is why the "Shadow of Loss" hypothesis needs genealogical data for *at least* three generations in the maternal line, and preferably four generations.

Reflections on loss

Loss is a subject we already know a lot about, not least from my father's third volume – "Loss: Sadness and Depression" (Bowlby, 1985) and from the work of his many colleagues (for example Colin Murray Parkes, 2010). Although many professionals understand and treat the painful impact of loss on a regular basis, society as a whole and, I suspect, many scientific researchers may have lost sight of its profound significance in family dynamics when children are very young.

For some time now, adverse attachment experiences in childhood have been linked to depression in adulthood, and more recent studies have linked adult depression with an increased risk of dementia. Might the risk of dementia sometimes depend on the very same experiences in childhood which predispose people to sadness and depression? Feeling helpless and hopeless in fearful situations is traumatic – should we be learning from the child survivors of genocide whose early trauma are impacting their mental and physical health many years later?

Where do we go from here?

I think understanding the nature of a problem holds out hope of a solution; lack of understanding tends to bring confusion and fatalistic hopelessness. The material outlined on attachment and loss and the possible link to dementia is sobering both at a personal and at a societal level. Most of us will have experienced loss of a loved-one at some time in our lives, and many of us will have known someone with dementia. Jane and I have been searching the literature for material that might align with her hypothesis, and she has written e-mails to the authors of relevant academic papers and books, attaching an informal report outlining her findings. We acknowledge that our literature search is incomplete, and the correspondence was limited to about 200 authors, but no-one to date has suggested that the model she is proposing cannot be accurate, and she has received some enthusiastic and very encouraging responses. However, it's becoming clear that the unconventional mind-set underpinning Jane's work does not fit easily within any established research programmes. Jane and I are agreed that the "Shadow of Loss" hypothesis and her informal research findings need to be thoroughly tested by independent academic research and the results of such studies should be published in peer review journals and online via *open access*.

Discussion

I have presented the main factors that seem to be associated with the "Shadow of Loss" hypothesis; there are many questions left unanswered.

Q.   What academic specialty would undertake a scientific study of this unconventional hypothesis?

A.   I think it would have to be collaboration between several relevant disciplines, as the *Shadow of Loss* hypothesis holds great potential for a thesis.

Q. What funding body would support scientific research in this field?

A. The problem is that most funding bodies want hard science with gold standard credentials – Jane and I are self-funded amateurs. Again, PhD students may be the way forward.

Q. How would one go about designing a study to test the *Shadow of Loss* hypothesis? And what psychological and physiological *mechanisms* might be involved associating the *Shadow of Loss* with dementia?

A. This is *really* not our field, but possible mechanisms might include:

- DNA and genetic susceptibility, for example ApoE4 gene
- epigenetic vulnerabilities, (stress/cortisol levels, HPA axis)
- impaired neurological development in infancy or childhood
- impaired glucose regulation
- altered neuropeptide functioning
- inflammation and immunological dysfunction
- chromosomal ageing of telomeres
- cognitive reserve and/or allostatic load

Q. What pre-symptomatic diagnostic technique for dementia might be developed?

A. Investigate the use of the Adult Attachment Interview before symptoms appear.

Q. What preventions or early interventions might reduce the risk of developing dementia?

A. Working with and supporting parents who have been bereaved during pregnancy or the early life of their baby and who have already lost someone close during their own childhood; and working with children, families and older individuals who are not managing to resolve their feelings following bereavement or other traumatic experience.

Q. What sort of care might be most appropriate for a person with dementia?

A. There are studies of non-familial care where the professional provider forms a genuine bond with the person who has dementia that seems to greatly relieve the symptoms of agitation and parent fixation. (*Simulated presence therapy* (Abraha et al., 2017) and the *Butterfly Approach* to dementia care as described by David Sheard and colleagues, (Sheard, 2013 and Knocker, 2015).

Acknowledgements

This chapter is based on a paper given at an international attachment conference in Los Angeles, UCLA held on 15 March 2014.

Thank you to Jane Sherwood for her diligent research on this important subject and her vital contribution to this chapter.

References

Abraha I, Rimland JM, Lozano-Montoya I, Dell'Aquila G, Vélez-Díaz-Pallarés M, Trotta FM, Cruz-Jentoft AJ, and Cherubini A. (2017). Simulated presence therapy for dementia. *Cochrane Database of Systematic Reviews*, Issue 4. Art. No.: CD011882. DOI: 10.1002/14651858.CD011882.pub2. www.cochranelibrary.com (accessed 16th July 2018).

Ainsworth, M., Blehar, M. C., Waters, E., & Wall, S. N. (1978, 2015). Strange situation procedure. *Patterns of Attachment: A Psychological Study of the Strange Situation*. London: Routledge.

Alzheimer's Society (2017). www.alzheimers.org.uk (accessed 17th October 2017).

Bowlby, J. (1985). *Loss: Sadness and Depression*. Harmondsworth: Penguin.

George, C., Kaplan, N., & Main, M., (1996). *Adult Attachment Interview*. Unpublished MS, Department of Psychology, University of California at Berkeley, third ed.

Håkansson, K., Rovio, S., Helkala, E., Vilska, A., Winblad, B., Soininen, H., Nissinen, A., Mohammed, A. H., & Kivipelto, M. (2009). Association between mid-life marital status and cognitive function in later life: population based cohort study. *British Medical Journal*, 339: b2462. doi: https://doi.org/10.1136/bmj.b2462

Knocker, S. (2015). *Loving, The Essence of Being a Butterfly in Dementia Care*. London: Hawker Publications.

Liotti G. (1992). Disorganized/disoriented attachment in the etiology of the dissociative disorders. *Dissociation*. 5: 196–204.

Muir, R. (1994). *The Trouble with Evan*. A documentary directed by Neil Docherty. Fifth Estate, CBC.

O'Leary, J., & Gaziano, C. (2011). The experience of adult siblings born after loss. *Attachment*, 5(3): 246–272.

Parkes, C. M. (2010). *Bereavement: Studies of Grief in Adult Life* (4th edition, with Holly Prigerson). London: Routledge.

Sheard, D. (2013). The feeling of mattering: The positioning of emotions in dementia care. *The Journal of Dementia Care*, 21(2): 23–27.

Schore, A. (1994). *Affect Regulation and the Origin of the Self: The Neurobiology of Emotional Development*. New York: Lawrence Erlbaum.

Sundström, A., Westerlund, O., Mousavi-Nasab, H., Adolfsson, R., & Nilsson, L. G. (2014). The relationship between marital and parental status and the risk of dementia. *International Psychogeriatrics*, 26(5): 749–757. doi: 10.1017/S1041610213002652.

Tschanz, J. T, Treiber, K., Norton, M. C., Welsh-Bohmer, K. A., Toone L., Zandi, P. P., & Breitner, J. C. (2005). A population study of Alzheimer's Disease: Findings from the Cache County Study on Memory, Health, and Aging. *Care Management Journal*, 6(2): 107–114.

Chapter 7

Dementia
Childhood attachment and loss

Jane Sherwood

In this informal pilot study, the cross-generational backgrounds of sixty people with late onset dementia were investigated and then compared with those of sixty people who retained all their mental faculties despite an elevated statistical risk of dementia in late life. Civil records dating back to 1837 were used to explore each person's family history for clues about the early experience of the generations who immediately preceded them. The differences which emerged between the two groups were striking, with the backgrounds of the dementia sample containing significantly more incidences of premature loss than those of the comparison group. The findings are described and analysed with particular regard to attachment theory.

Introduction

Relatives and front-line care staff often notice a history of trauma in the lives of people with dementia. Enquiries into the lives of an initial ad hoc sample of fifty-one people with dementia revealed what appeared to be unusually high levels of childhood loss, particularly the death of fathers. (See Figure 7.1 for the composition of this initial cluster of fifty-one people.) I employed a pie diagram to make sense of the unexpected picture which I found emerging.

That so many people with dementia had fathers who died during their childhood was particularly surprising. (It also alerted me to the possible significance of other childhood losses and separations.) At least some of the paternal deaths were known to have occurred, for example, as a result of industrial accidents rather than from medical conditions which might nowadays be suspected of having some relevance to the offspring's long-term health. An association between early paternal death and increased dementia risk is supported by the findings of the Cache County Study on Memory, Health and Ageing (N = 1793) led by Dr Maria Norton, which found that the loss of fathers before the age of 5 years tripled the risk of dementia. (Norton et al., 2009)

I was not convinced that material hardship and loss of status following a father's death satisfactorily accounted for the apparent association between paternal death and an elevated dementia risk. My long career as a social worker taught me that

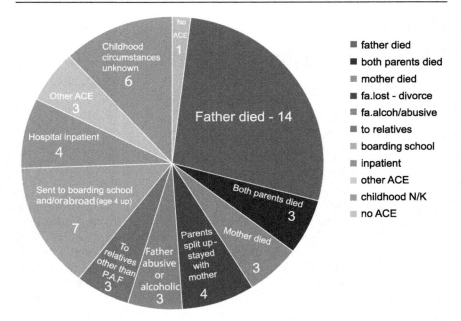

Figure 7.1 Adverse Childhood Experience amongst 51 people with dementia

Note:

PAF: Primary Attachment Figure

ACE: Adverse Childhood Experience

some children receive high quality care from parents who lack material resources, while other children fail to have their needs met at all well despite considerable affluence and social prestige. Furthermore, were material hardship, low status and possible stigma key factors here? One would expect the impact of being born to unmarried parents to increase the dementia risk in at least equal measure to premature paternal death. I have found no research identifying birth outside marriage as a risk factor for dementia. Something else appears to be going on.

I eventually decided to reframe the various categories of adverse childhood experience (ACE Study, Fellitti, et al., 1998) which I had identified, as shown in Figure 7.2.

Thirty-nine of my original ad hoc fifty-one people had researchable British origins, and I was gradually able to bring my sample size from this initial thirty-nine up to forty-five as new names became known to me.

An instance of particularly severe mothering in one of these early cases led me to research the mother's own background for clues as to its origins. This was enlightening, and it alerted me to the potential usefulness of investigating the backgrounds of the other forty-four people's parents too.

A pattern started to emerge of what were, in my genealogical experience, uncommonly high levels of childhood bereavement in the early lives of my sample's parents and grandparents. Most striking was the compound nature of the

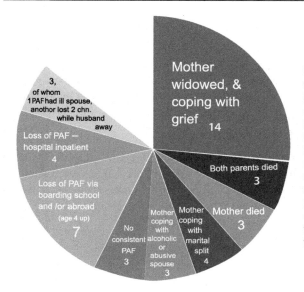

Revised wording shows that 44 people out of the initial 51 with dementia can be seen as having lacked a fully available Primary Attachment Figure in childhood– someone who was always present, and in a reasonable position to provide a high level of emotional support throughout the child's formative years

Figure 7.2 Lack of consistently available primary attachment figure

childhood bereavements suffered across two or more generations by many fami-lies in this study. From an attachment theory perspective, few amongst this infor-mal sample of people with dementia had backgrounds conducive to receiving early security of attachment to a primary attachment figure. Secure early attach-ment has elsewhere been shown to be a prerequisite for emotional resilience in adult life, particularly in the face of trauma (Holmes, 2017).

Despite this being an unfunded project, I then decided similar research was needed into the cross-generational backgrounds of a carefully selected compari-son group, albeit again an informal one. By now, my dementia sample had swelled to fifty-five.

I made requests in my home community, to all likely e-mail contacts, and to Family History Society groups in the county where I live and its neighbour, for the names of fifty-five people, born in the twentieth century, who remained dementia free despite:

• having lived to over 80 years
• and having been widowed, divorced or never having been married
• and having lived alone at the end of their life
• and, if possible, having themselves cared for a spouse with dementia.

After an unpromising start, a sudden rush of responses provided sixty suitable names. Rather than distort the randomness of the comparison group by filtering any nominees out, I successfully appealed to my most recent informants for fur-ther names to bring the dementia sample up to a corresponding sixty in total.

The original group of fifty-one with dementia about whose lives I had been able to gather some basic information had been taken from UK and US Alzheimer's websites, or from biographical material in the public domain as well as from any private informants who could help me. The sample was therefore random but not randomised. No more than one person was included in the study from any genetic line, even when there had been more than one instance of dementia in the family.

The composition of the two groups

Although premature loss tends to be dismissed as a common feature of life in Britain in the nineteenth and early twentieth century, it became very clear from my genealogical researches that some families were far more affected than others by the ravages of industrialisation and urbanisation.

Factors such as:

- long hours in harsh working environments
- low pay and inadequate nutrition
- overcrowded living conditions
- infectious disease
- unsafe urban water supplies
- minimal education

trapped many people in poverty and increased their risk of dying prematurely.

My findings led me to wonder if the inequalities of Victorian society might now be distorting our perception of the causes of dementia. Low socio-economic status and limited education, for instance, have been linked to a heightened risk of dementia but these are both characteristics associated with lack of opportunity in preceding generations.

The 120 people in this study came from various social backgrounds, but I was not in a position systematically to match them according to socio-economic status. I was, however, able to maximise the late life risk of dementia in the comparison group according to established research on age, marital status, lone living etc. As will be seen from Figure 7.3, the late life risk of dementia within the comparison group exceeded that in the dementia sample on all such criteria.

Marital status and dementia risk

Having a living spouse has consistently been found by recent research to confer significant protection against dementia. Persson and Skoog (1996), however, found married status more common in the thirty-eight people in their prospective study who developed dementia than in the 336 who remained dementia free. (Their sample of 374 represented a carefully randomised subset of everyone in the local population register who had been born in a particular year.) Nevertheless, eighteen of the dementia sample (30 percent) had living spouses. None of the comparison group had this protection at the end of their lives.

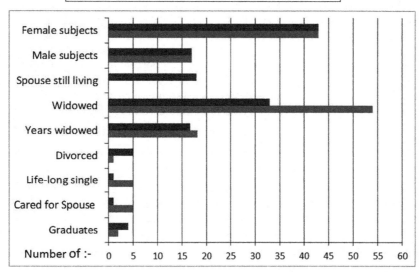

Figure 7.3

Having had a spouse with dementia, in later life, has been linked with a significant increase in the risk of dementia (e.g. six-fold in one large community study). Two people in the dementia sample had experienced their partner having dementia, although one of them – the man – had had nothing at all to do with providing any care for his wife (when she had cancer in mid-life or) when she developed Alzheimer's Disease (AD). Four people in the comparison group (two men and two women) had had spouses with dementia and had cared for them.

There were thirty-one widows/widowers in the dementia sample and fifty-four in the comparison group, and they were widowed for an average of sixteen years and seven months and eighteen years two months respectively. Two of the dementia sample had been widowed twice, as had one in the comparison group.

Widowers were markedly less common than widows in both groups, and were widowed for less time. The six widowers in the dementia sample had been widowed for an average of twelve years and two months, with two of them developing dementia within three years of their wives' deaths. The seventeen widowers in the comparison group were widowed for an average of thirteen and a half years.

Only one person in the dementia sample was single, compared with five in the comparison group.

For divorced people, the position was reversed, with there being only one divorced woman in the comparison group but five in the dementia sample (four women, one man). All six divorced people had spent the vast majority of their adult lives without a spouse.

Nine out of only seventeen men with dementia in my study (i.e. 53 percent of all men in the dementia sample) were married when their dementia manifested – as must surely have been the additional man who died of Alzheimer's disease (AD) only a year after losing his wife. The number of married women with dementia was also nine, but they formed only 21 percent of the forty-three women in the sample. Another way of looking at this is that men formed 50 percent of the married dementia subjects despite constituting only twenty-two of the whole dementia sample. These findings do not seem at variance with those of the large community study in Cache County – summarised in Figure 7.4 – and I think they raise some important new questions.

2,442 subjects (1,221 married couples) aged sixty-five and older from Northern Utah, USA, without dementia at onset, were studied for up to twelve years to monitor for onset of dementia in husbands, wives or both.

During this time:

- 125 cases of dementia only in the husband were diagnosed
- seventy only in the wife, and
- thirty where both spouses were diagnosed (sixty people).

The researchers, led by Dr Maria Norton of Utah State University, USA, adjusted for socioeconomic status, a significant predictor of many health-related outcomes including dementia, to control for shared environmental exposures that might influence risk for dementia in both spouses.

Figure 7.4

When compared to the men with dementia in my study, the women with dementia were:

- older
- much more likely to have suffered the loss of their marital partner
- more likely be a widow, and widowed for longer
- less likely to have Alzheimer's Disease (AD) as their particular form of dementia
- particularly unlikely to have both AD and a spouse

There have always been, and remain, complications affecting the definitive diagnosis of Alzheimer's Disease, even post mortem. The low rate of confirmed

	TOTAL	MALES	FEMALES
No. of people with dementia	60 (100%)	17 (28%)	43 (72%)
No. married	18 (30%)	9 (15%)	9 (15%)
No. with definite AD	15 (25%)	10 (17%)	5 (8%)
Married, & with AD	9 (15%)	7 (12%)	2 (3%)
No. widowed	32 (53%)	6 (10%)	26 (43%)
Percentage of all widow/ers	100%	19%	81%
Average time widowed	16yrs 8mths	12yrs 1mth	18yrs
Average age (at onset if known/death if not)	82yrs 5mths	80yrs 11mths	83yrs 3mths

Figure 7.5 Gender within the dementia sample

AD to other dementias in my sample was likely to be a function of significant under diagnosis, but there is no reason why under diagnosis should have applied unequally across the sexes.

I note that Persson and Skoog (1996), found that slightly fewer women (eighteen) than men (twenty) in their prospective study developed dementia between the age of 70 and 79 years, although the ratio of women to men in their study was 219:155 i.e. approximately four to three (Persson & Skoog, 1996).

Age remains the single best predictor of dementia risk

The mean age of the dementia sample, either at death (the vast majority) or currently, was 82 years and 5 months – but this is an over-estimate relative to that of the comparison group, as dementia has been shown to affect people for an average of five to seven years before they die. The mean age of the comparison group was calculated from the ages at which fifty-six of the group had died, together with the current ages of the four living people in the group, all of who were lively-minded nonagenarians managing in the community despite, in some instances, now having awkward combinations of sensory and physical disabilities. (Two of these four nonagenarians have since died, still completely free of dementia.) One person, for instance, with no relatives or neighbours to assist her, continued to manage solitary living despite being registered blind for several years and now losing her hearing. The mean age in the comparison group came out at 88 years and 2 months (range 80 to 102 years).

Education is seen as protective against dementia

However, the dementia sample contained four graduates, three of whom were women (i.e. exceptionally high achievers for their era). There were only two graduates, a woman and a man in the comparison group.

Family size

Victoria Moceri, at the University of Washington in 2001, carried out a study of 770 people aged 60 and older who were members of a large health maintenance organisation in Seattle. Of the participants, 393 had Alzheimer's disease and 377 had no signs of dementia.

Every additional child in any family was found to increase the Alzheimer's risk of the sibling set by 8 percent. This increase in risk was attributed to large families being more likely to come from lower socioeconomic levels, and therefore to be more likely to have children with poor (brain) growth rates. I found no similar link with larger families, even amongst the confirmed instances of AD rather than other forms of dementia (see Figure 7.6).

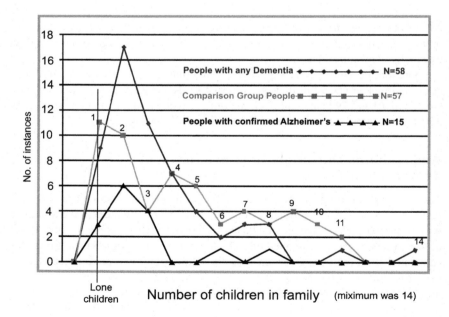

Figure 7.6

Higher paternal age at conception

This has been found to increase the risk of gene mutations which compromise the offspring's brain. The fathers of the people in the comparison group were at least as old as those of the dementia sample. The differences between the two groups cannot therefore be attributed to any higher paternal age at conception within the dementia sample (see Figure 7.7).

High maternal age at delivery

This was similarly found significant by Persson and Skoog (1996), but not in my study (see Figure 7.8).

Comparative results

A striking difference emerged between the two groups in that the dementia sample had suffered significantly more premature bereavement across recent generations than had the comparison group.

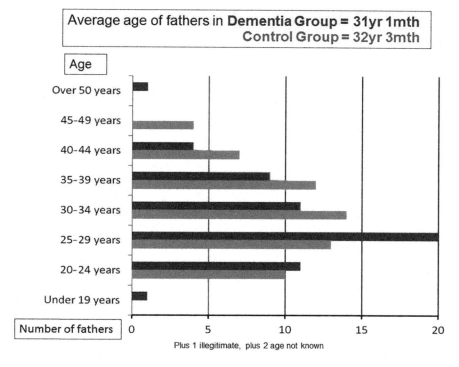

Figure 7.7

AVERAGE MATERNAL AGE AT TIME OF SUBJECT'S BIRTH

Comparison Group = 29yrs 5 mths   **Dementia Group = 28yrs 5 mths**

RANGE OF MATERNAL AGES AT TIME OF SUBJECT'S BIRTH

Comparison Group = 21yrs to 45yrs   **Dementia Group = 18yrs to 42yrs**

No teenagers	1 teenager
34 in their 20s	41 in their 20s
23 in their 30s	15 in their 30s
3 in their 40s (40yrs, 40yrs & 45yrs)	3 in their 40s (40yrs, 40yrs & 41yrs)

Figure 7.8

LOSS OF PRIMARY ATTACHMENT FIGURE (PAF) DURING CHILDHOOD

COMPARISON GROUP PEOPLE (CGP) N=60	PEOPLE WITH DEMENTIA (PWD) N=60
Age at time of mother's death	*Age at time of mother's death*
0 (raised by maternal aunt & uncle. Birth father died when 11)	2.75yrs (T.B.-mother progressively ill beforehand)
7.5yrs	3yrs
8yrs	7yrs (T.B.-which then killed father when child 13yrs)
9yrs	8yrs
	13yrs
	14yrs (then chronically ill father died within 6mths.)

EARLY CHILDHOOD SEPARATIONS FROM PAFs

1 CGP was placed in a convent for safety during WW1 in Europe & then her father died when she was 14	1 PWD went abroad to boarding school aged 8yrs
1 CGP's mother spent 30yrs in an asylum from when CGP was 3.75yrs	1 PWD was evacuated during WW2, aged 10yrs
1 CGP went into care aged 6 beacause mother couldn't cope with her large family	1 PWD went to severe grandmother, aged 14mths when next, frail, sibling was born
	4 PWD were hosipital inpatients for up to several months

Figure 7.9

Jane Sherwood, 2013

Western society, I feel, has become blasé about the personal impact of high infant (and adult) mortality in the nineteenth and early twentieth century. There is no good reason to presume that a Victorian woman who lost a child felt any less distress than a grief-stricken woman feels today. She may well have had less

LOSS OF FATHERS DURING CHILDHOOD

COMPARISON GROUP PEOPLE N=60

Age at time of father's death
1yr
11yrs (aftermother died at birth.
Raised by maternal aunt & uncle).
12.75yrs
14yrs

PEOPLE WITH DEMENTIA N=60

Age at time of father's death
1yr
2yrs
3yrs
6yrs
7yrs (ww1 casualty)
8yrs
9yrs
13yrs (T.B. -child's mother already dead)
15yrs (chronically ill & recently widowed)
16yrs (progressive, debilitating illness)
18yrs
19yrs (chronically ill)

LONG TERM PATERNAL ABSENCES

1 other father served in WW1
  whilst CGP was under 5yrs

5 other fathers served in WW1 or
  WW2 while PWD were under 5yrs
2 other fathers served in WW1 or
  WW2 from when PWD were 6-8yrs old
2 other fathers deserted their famillies (one
  when PWD was 4, the other when PWD was 12)

Figure 7.10
Jane Sherwood, 2013

opportunity to grieve, however. In the backgrounds of 120 people in this study, I came across women who had lost as many as eleven children. One unrecognised implication of infant mortality on such a scale is that some surviving children would have experienced their primary attachment figure as recently-bereaved through much of their early life. Some of the Seattle results on family size, referred to previously, surprised the researchers. A different way of looking at large families is that the statistical risk of a young mother encountering the loss of a child increases with each new infant born to her.

It was suggested that I try using my social work knowledge and experience of the impact of broken attachments to apply a simple ten-point scale to the number and severity of the childhood losses in the backgrounds of the maternal line of each of the 120 people in my study. It was not possible to carry out this exercise blind, nor did I have a collaborator who could cross-check the scores I allocated, so I erred on the side of generosity when scoring any rather limited information about the backgrounds of people in the comparison group. For example, I would assume a lost child in those instances when there was a gap in sibling births but no viable way of confirming a correct date of birth and death. A team approach will be needed to establish a reliable scale for future use. This was just an initial effort to convey, in visual form, the striking differences I had been noticing amongst the family trees I had drawn up. I was guided by the following parameters:

- Backgrounds where there had been no bereavements during the early life of the individual in my study, or of their mother, or of their maternal grandmother, scored zero.
- Backgrounds scored nine where the catalogue of childhood losses/separations was so extreme that it was hard to imagine how any further tragedies could have made early life significantly worse.
- All the remaining backgrounds were ranked in relation to these two extreme scores and to each other.

Figure 7.11 shows the overall results of this trial exercise in quantifying transgenerational attachment issues. It will be noted that:

- Eighty percent of the comparison group scored three or less (below the dotted line), whereas 91 percent of the dementia group scored four or more (above the dotted line)
- Twelve people (20 percent) in the comparison group had *no* identifiable instances of early loss in their backgrounds so scored zero, as against only one person in the dementia sample.

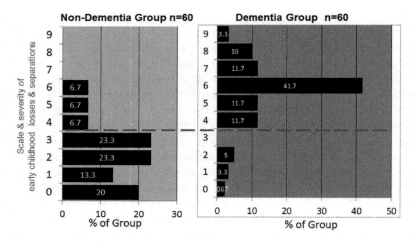

Figure 7.11 Bereavements and separations in early life likely to impact on security of attachment: a social work assessment based on official records spanning four generations

Jane Sherwood, 2013. Provisional review of data only

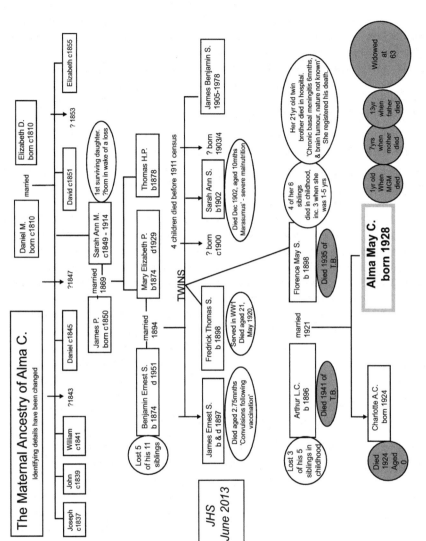

The Maternal Ancestry of Alma C.
Identifying details have been changed

Daniel M. born c1810 — married — Elizabeth D. born c1810

Joseph c1837 | John c1839 | William c1841 | ?1843 | Daniel c1845 | ?1847 | David c1851 | ?1853 | Elizabeth c1855

James P. born c1850 — married 1869 — Sarah Ann M. c1849 – 1914

1st surviving daughter. ?born in wake of a loss

Benjamin Ernest S. b 1874 d 1951 — married 1894 — Mary Elizabeth P. b1874 d1929

Thomas H.P. b1878

Lost 5 of his 11 siblings

4 children died before 1911 census

James Ernest S. b & d 1897

Died aged 2.75mnths 'Convulsions following vaccination'

Fredrick Thomas S. b 1898

Served in WW1 Died aged 21, May 1920.

TWINS

? born c1900

? born 1903/4

Sarah Ann S. b1902

Died Dec 1902, aged 10mths Marasmus' - severe malnutrition

James Benjamin S. 1905-1978

Florence May S. b 1898 — married 1921 — Arthur L.C. b 1896

Died 1935 of T.B.

Died 1941 of T.B.

4 of her 6 siblings died in childhood, inc. 3 when she was 1-5 yrs

Her 21yr old twin brother died in hospital. 'Chronic basal meningitis 6mnths; & brain tumour, nature not known' She registered his death.

Lost 3 of his 5 siblings in childhood

Charlotte A.C. born 1924

Died 1924 Aged 0

Alma May C. born 1928

1yr old When MGM died | 7yrs when mother died | 13yr when father died | Widowed at 63

JHS June 2013

Figure 7.12

There were only two backgrounds which scored the maximum nine, both from the dementia sample rather than the comparison group.

Figure 7.12, entitled "The maternal ancestry of Alma C", is a selective family tree illustrating a combined personal and maternal *early* background which I scored at 9 on a 0–9 scale of attachment traumas. The fact that the subject encountered widowhood in her sixties was not taken into account when scoring, as this was a late-life event. (For the sake of completeness I later investigated two earlier generations than are shown here.)

One of the two instances of a person with dementia whose own/maternal background was scored at nine (identifying details have been changed).

Resilience in the comparison group

The highest-scoring people in the comparison group, i.e. those whose backgrounds were allocated a score of six, all achieved this on account of having had some childhood experience of institutional care.

It might be relevant, though, that three of them were at least six years old by the time of their residential admission so they may have experienced some secure attachment within their families until that point.

One of these three children also had the good fortune to be cared for in a Family Group Home by a kindly housemother (i.e. who provided the experience of a primary attachment figure) with whom he kept in touch in adulthood.

The fourth person, the one whose time of admission is not known, suffered an impersonal and probably punitive workhouse upbringing consequent upon her bigamous father's failure to support his second wife and family.

The resilience of the high-scorers in the comparison group is interesting and it may in time prove significant that they all had siblings who suffered the same fate as they did.

When I was considering the concept that the burying of traumatic memory might constitute a route into dementia with the son of one of the sample, he commented that his father and numerous uncles and aunts had had the advantage of being able to complain heartily to each other about their childhood experience whenever they met at family gatherings over the years because their father was profoundly deaf and couldn't hear what they were saying(!).

Having someone to believe and validate one's traumatic experience is an essential part of the healing process. Siblings may, at least sometimes, be able to help each other keep painful memories within conscious awareness rather than feel obliged to bury them.

The number of singletons viz-a-viz eldest siblings, youngest siblings etc. did not appear significantly different in the dementia sample than in the comparison group.

These high scores in the comparison group could, of course, be a function of over-generous scoring of instances of separation (rather than permanent loss) on my part. My generous scoring of separations, though, was influenced by my knowledge that, out of my original fifty-one people with dementia:

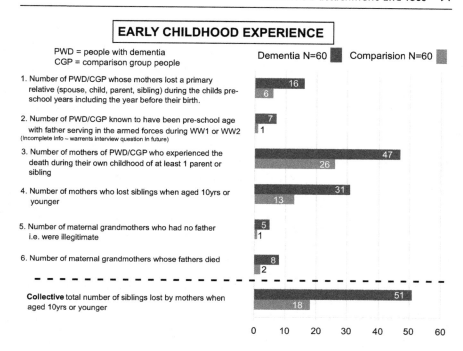

EARLY CHILDHOOD EXPERIENCE

PWD = people with dementia
CGP = comparison group people

Dementia N=60 ■   Comparision N=60 ■

1. Number of PWD/CGP whose mothers lost a primary relative (spouse, child, parent, sibling) during the childs pre-school years including the year before their birth.   16 / 6

2. Number of PWD/CGP known to have been pre-school age with father serving in the armed forces during WW1 or WW2 (Incomplete info – warrents interview question in future)   7 / 1

3. Number of mothers of PWD/CGP who experienced the death during their own childhood of at least 1 parent or sibling   47 / 26

4. Number of mothers who lost siblings when aged 10yrs or younger   31 / 13

5. Number of maternal grandmothers who had no father i.e. were illegitimate   5 / 1

6. Number of maternal grandmothers whose fathers died   8 / 2

Collective total number of siblings lost by mothers when aged 10yrs or younger   51 / 18

0   10   20   30   40   50   60

Figure 7.13

- Ten had experienced separations in childhood, often reportedly highly trau-matic, which were occasioned by being sent to boarding school – sometimes in another country – and/or to live away from the relatives with whom they started life.
- Four others (all of whom had British backgrounds so went on to figure in my dementia sample) had coped, unaccompanied by a familiar adult, with child-hood in-patient hospital stays and distressing treatments in an era of very limited parental visiting.
- Three others had been raised by unsupported mothers following parental dis-harmony and eventual marital breakdown.

The importance of timing

Comparative information about the timing of key bereavements in the lives of mothers of the 120 people in my study is shown in Figure 7.13. Paternal back-grounds were equally tragic, but I had noticed very early on, from the backgrounds of my original fifty-one names of people with dementia, that the common factor in the vast majority of their histories was an early lack of uninterrupted "mother-ing". By this, I mean that the events in their childhoods were such that they were unlikely to have experienced uninterrupted early care from their primary attach-ment figure (PAF).

Information about maternal grandmothers' childhoods is harder to obtain. Deaths in England and Wales are currently indexed only by name until the 1870s, with no reference to the deceased person's age. Without purchasing enormous numbers of speculative death certificates, costing over nine pounds each, lost siblings of maternal grandmothers (MGMs) born in the nineteenth century are particularly difficult to identify accurately. Maternal grandmothers in the two groups could nevertheless be traced as having lost a similar number of mothers as each other in childhood, namely:

- Five MGMs in the comparison group lost their mothers, at birth, and at the ages of 3, 3¾, between 12 and 13, and between 13 and 14 respectively.
- Seven MGMs in the dementia group lost their mothers, at the ages of 3, 8, between 9 and 12, 10, 13 and two at the age of 17 respectively. (I have included the 17-year-olds because teenage loss of mother has been linked with a heightened risk of AD – as identified in the Cache County Study, Norton et al., 2009.)

There was a striking difference, though, between the fathering/supported mothering experienced in childhood by the two groups of maternal grandmothers. Significantly more MGMs in the dementia sample were born out of wedlock or had fathers die than in the comparison group (see Figure 7.13).

The bereaved primary attachment figure

A child's primary attachment figure (PAF) is most commonly, but not necessarily, the biological mother. For the sake of clarity, I shall refer to the PAF as mother/"she", and her child as "he".

The task facing a recently bereaved mother is an unenviable one. There is no ideal way for her to shield her young children from the potential fall-out of the tragedy which has befallen her. If she has a history of unresolved childhood loss, this is likely to complicate her ability to mourn effectively. *Loss: Sadness and Depression*, the final part of John Bowlby's (1980) trilogy, *Attachment and Loss*, remains one of the most useful texts for helping us understand the devastating impact of the death of a loved one.

- The mother tries to behave as if nothing has happened, her children are likely to sense that this is not so – especially in the years before they become skilled at using and understanding language. Sudden, inexplicable, changes in parental behaviour confuse and easily frighten children. The younger the child, the fewer defensive strategies he will have at his disposal. Painful feelings which go unrecognised and remain unresolved in the absence of sensitive adult intervention all too easily get buried. Defensive patterns quickly become set – and handed down within the family.
- A mother who has lost her husband is in a particularly complex situation. If she tries to be reasonably open with her feelings, or ever breaks down in front

of her young child(ren), they are likely to fear losing their surviving parent and have fears of being abandoned. Children's typical fears in situations such as these were not recognised and understood until the mid-twentieth century. A father's death (or absence due to wartime front-line service) also deprives his wife of key emotional support just when she and, through her, their young children are likely to need it most.

- If it is a child who has died, the surviving siblings can readily mistake their mother's grief as indicating that she loved her lost child more, and that their own feelings are relatively unimportant to her. This is another route to children learning to dismiss their own feelings.
- If a mother is open about what has happened but covers up her distress about it, this is what her young children will, by example and by the firing of mirror neurons, learn to do the same thing in similarly painful emotional circumstances. They will thereby potentially store up a catalogue of unprocessed traumatic experiences throughout life.
- The inclination to cry is particularly problematic for mothers and young children alike. Any mother who is trying to stifle a need to weep will find it very difficult to respond with anything like her usual sensitivity and generosity of spirit to the need for constant closeness, reassurance and encouragement during the clinging, tears and tantrums which characterise normal toddlerhood. Children, for their part, are keen to please their caregivers, and the natural and healthy inclination to cry can easily be lost. Several of my informants separately commented that their relative/friend with dementia was never able to cry.
- Without sensitive and sympathetic early handling of their emotions, children are in danger of learning that their feelings are of no value, and thus grow up disconnected from them. Learning not to feel anger, for instance, invites exploitation and can easily produce depression. Shared roots in early childhood adversity could help account for the connection between depression and dementia, although the biological model has so far presumed straightforward cause-and-effect between depression and dementia. Lifelong disconnection from one's feelings might also explain why Alzheimer's Disease can seem to reintroduce people to "lost" parts of their personality. For example, with people who were mild or submissive becoming able to show their anger and asking for their needs to be met, or those who always seemed "tough" being reduced to unexpected anxiety or tears.

These are just some of the ways in which death within the close family can impact on young children's emotional development, and on the ways in which they will habitually handle difficult feelings in adulthood.

Resilience and optimism

Recently there has been considerable investigation into resilience, especially amongst people who have been bereaved. For example, see the work of George Bonanno and colleagues (Bonanno, 2005, Pressman, et. al, 2007). Most adults can be shown to make a satisfactory recovery from bereavement without outside intervention (although good social support is beneficial). Optimism, likewise, has been receiving a great deal of academic attention, and has been shown to benefit the neuronal connections within the brain. Neither the work on resilience nor the work on optimism, however, disproves that there may be unseen, very long-term consequences of finding ways of avoiding fully registering and processing grief. Compulsive self-reliance, developed as a coping strategy in childhood but leaving the adult emotionally vulnerable, can all too easily be mistaken for true resilience.

When someone shuts out troubling feelings without even noticing them occurring, their distressing experiences remain unprocessed. Keeping busy can be a useful distraction against feeling and introspection (which may contribute to its usefulness as an apparent protection against dementia). But traumatic memories may become harder to keep buried as the years pass.

There were certainly people in my dementia sample who were exceptionally good at keeping up their spirits throughout life, even when faced with bereavement. But the experience of sadness has its place in allowing us to move on in a healthy way after tragedy strikes. A healthy way is one that does not expose us to the risk of later converting unprocessed traumatic experience into physical or psychological expressions of dis-ease. The current pervasiveness of dementia may itself be suggesting we need to review how we can best integrate the experience of interpersonal loss and other traumas.

The relevance of a secure base

Some of the biological changes associated with dementia are also associated with insecure attachment or trauma. Altered immunity, altered cortisol responsiveness, altered gene expression, altered glucose regulation, and altered neuropeptide functioning are just a few examples of this. The concepts of allostatic load and cognitive reserve are central to current thinking about dementia, and they too may conceivably be affected by attachment traumas which are particularly ill-timed. The lack of a secure base (Bowlby, 1979) and the inability to regulate one's emotions can result in painful feelings being habitually but unconsciously kept out of awareness, which is known to be injurious to long-term physical as well as mental health.

The lack of a secure base is not generally identifiable without detailed and highly skilled assessment, but factors such as relationship breakdown and mental illness are likely indicators. Post-Traumatic Stress Disorder (PTSD), like clinical depression/Major Depressive Disorder (MDD), has been linked with both a heightened risk of dementia and also with adverse childhood experience.

Around 40 percent of the population are thought to lack a secure base but, in common with the population at large, not all 40 percent will survive long enough to be at serious risk of dementia.

The commonly occurring behaviours known as parent fixation and parent orientation are taken to represent efforts by people with dementia to re-capture the security enjoyed in early childhood, but my findings lead me to suspect they may actually represent renewed, desperate attempts to elicit a security of attachment that never was. It is interesting that the principles of attachment theory are increasingly being applied in dementia care settings, with encouraging results. Why should these principles make a significant difference to problems that are not somehow attachment based?

We need to be very careful, though, to check the context of expressed desires such as "to go home because my mother's expecting me". I asked the daughter of a nursing home resident who had started expressing such a desire, if her mother had perhaps cared for her grandmother in later life? The answer was immediately that she had done, for very many years. Maybe what this resident, and some others, was expressing here was an anxiety about the wellbeing of an aged parent who used to depend on her. Children whose early attachment needs were poorly met can also grow up feeling overly responsible for the care of others.

Late-life stress

Late life tends to bring particular challenges to attachment security. The longer someone lives, the more bereavements s/he is likely to encounter. Not only does each bereavement constitute a personal loss but it also depletes the number of potential attachment figures who might offer support in adversity – a potential "safe haven". Some of the particular late-life challenges which came to my attention in the context of my dementia enquiries were:

* Recent widowhood
* Imminent loss of one's partner
* Intrusive memories of trauma, without access to sufficiently effective distraction
* Sudden indications that a spouse is vulnerable, or a reminder that s/he is mortal
* The particularly traumatic loss of a loved one e.g. by suicide, or accident or in another country
* Loss of one's child or grandchild
* An unfortunate cluster of losses of close family members
* For those living alone, the imminent loss of a last surviving sibling/friend/ neighbour
* A hospital in-patient episode, especially if such an instance had also occurred in early life
* The failure of one's partner to provide reciprocal care when needed, or retirement looming with an unsympathetic or hostile partner

Not everyone with an insecure base who survives into late old age will have the misfortune to encounter traumatic experiences such as these. But I have come to think that people who have grown up without adult help to tolerate and process painful feelings (i.e. effective emotion regulation) can find the extreme sadness or fear generated by late life events such as these, overwhelming or unbearable. Accumulated tragedy and early loss across recent generations may well conspire to deprive children of adequate positive experience of early attachment to see them safely through a long life which happens to have a significant emotional challenge at its end.

The scope to intervene

Trauma is already being overcome in other fields, and without the overwhelming horror of it needing to be re-experienced. So too are the remnants of actual or threatened personal loss, such as emotional overwhelm, disordered mourning, or fear for one's survival – which I am suggesting collectively may be the triggers for dementia.

It is likely to be impossible to prove that someone would have had dementia were it not for a given intervention. Nevertheless, if my findings are replicated, a sensible approach might be for anyone who finds their memory letting them down to consider seeking skilled therapeutic help to explore what fears, memories or uncomfortable feelings their subconscious mind may be struggling – by increasingly desperate means – to keep out of their conscious awareness.

Mind, body and spirit still tend to be dealt with in Western society as separate entities. Remarkably little time and interest is given to the part played by psychological factors in the creation of illness. The experience of dementia is recognised as seriously undermining to people's confidence in their own abilities and their sense of security. My social work perception, though, based on published case studies and research findings as well as on my own experience, is that dementia often seems to follow in the wake of destabilising changes in circumstance, if not more overt trauma.

Implications for future research and for social policy

From a cross-cultural perspective, might the changes brought about by industrialisation and urbanisation have increased the incidence of disordered mourning/burying of painful feelings – thereby helping to fuel current high dementia rates in the developed world? Lower rates of dementia in less developed countries are often put down to lack of awareness/diagnosis/reporting. Is it chance, though, that India has particularly low levels of Alzheimer's Disease, even allowing for the low incidence there of the ApoE4 allele? Or might the majority Indian religion, Hinduism, be providing just the kind of framework which people need in order to recover from personal bereavement i.e. an expectation that the grief-stricken should be encouraged to express their emotions, and be given practical support while they attend to doing so? Other indigenous peoples likewise have retained beliefs and practices which respect and restore emotional and spiritual wellbeing after loss and other traumas.

From an epidemiological perspective, was it just chance/cohort effect that I came across a high proportion of people with dementia who were very young children during one or other of the world wars, with absent fathers whose wives had tragic early backgrounds which were likely to render them uncommonly vulnerable emotionally? Future research needs to allow for the possibility that being a young child in wartime circumstances such as these might hold some relevance to late life dementia risk.

When I reviewed the birth timings of my two groups against the timing of the two World Wars (1914–1918 and 1939–1945), the only striking difference was in the period 1900–1910, when just three of the sixty people with dementia were born as against twenty-two people in the comparison group. The case examples I have come across suggest we may need to be alert to the particularly unfortunate timing for young children of emotionally vulnerable mothers in World War One, who then went on to experience an especially traumatic World War Two as adults. Likewise, young children whose fathers came back particularly damaged emotionally by their World War One military experience, and those young children who were separated from both their parents during the evacuation of British cities in World War Two may, under my analysis, be especially vulnerable to dementia. In some countries, including the UK, the dementia rate is now falling. Childhoods spent relatively safely between the two World Wars could be relevant to this, reinforcing the need to pay special attention to the precise choice of birth cohort in future research.

Contrary to government expectation, if my analysis is correct the "Baby Boom" generation of people who were born in Britain in the wake of the Second World War may well be *less* vulnerable to dementia than their immediate predecessors, because:

- Post-war children by definition had fathers who survived the conflict
- The nutrition and therefore the physical resilience of all children benefitted from the post-World War Two introduction of free daily pasteurised milk, and of subsidised meals in all state schools
- Child deaths/sibling losses fell as children started to be vaccinated against highly infectious diseases such as polio, diphtheria and scarlet fever
- The National Health Service began in 1948, making free treatment available to all, including new antibiotics
- The rate at which young adults/parents were dying fell drastically after World War Two in response to additional factors such as mass screening for tuberculosis coupled with the discovery of streptomycin

Recent findings that cancer and Alzheimer's, and arthritis and Alzheimer's, rarely occur together are taken to indicate that cancer and arthritis must somehow "protect" against Alzheimer's. Another way of looking at cancer, or arthritis, or Alzheimer's – or, for that matter, heart attacks, or strokes, or autoimmune diseases, or organ failure – is that each represents a response to a different type of stress. Why should we expect any more than one of them to occur in an organism trying to restore homeostasis in the face of a particular and distinct form of external or internal threat? We also might do well to question why poor cardiovascular health has been linked with an increased risk of Alzheimer's yet somehow fails to provide welcome and swift relief for the person with Alzheimer's via a fatal heart attack or stroke.

In my study, four of the people with dementia had already survived cancer in mid/late life. Interestingly, three of them not only had AD despite already having had cancer, but they were amongst only nine people with AD in my study who still had a living spouse.

Gender and marital status

The findings of my pilot study, coupled with those of the community-based Cache County Study (Norton et al., 2009), suggest there are some new questions we need to start asking about dementia in the context of gender and marital status.

- Despite the known higher prevalence of dementia amongst elderly women than amongst elderly men, (Hofman et al., 1991), out of 1,221 retired married couples followed up over a twelve-year period in Cache County (Norton et al., 2009), 125 husbands developed dementia but only seventy wives. (There were also thirty couples where both spouses developed dementia, but it is unclear to me in which order.)
- Men who had a spouse with dementia were found by the Cache County study (Norton et al., 2009), to have an 11.9 percent increased risk of dementia themselves, against an increased risk of only 3.7 percent for women who had a spouse with dementia.
- People with Alzheimer's represented only 25 percent (N = 15) of my dementia sample but 50 percent (N = 9) of those where there was a living spouse.
- There is no good reason to suppose Alzheimer's is diagnosed more frequently in one sex than the other. **I found, though, that my dementia sample contained twice as many men (N = 10) with Alzheimer's as women (N = 5)** although men represented only 28 percent of my overall dementia sample.
- Men with dementia in my study were found to be *almost ten times* as likely as women with dementia to have AD despite being married. Men accounted for seven of the nine people who had AD whilst married, whilst representing only 28 percent (N = 17) of the overall dementia sample. Women accounted for only two of the nine married people with AD whilst representing 72 percent of the overall dementia sample. Elsewhere, however, research has found that men looking after wives with dementia tend to be coping with a greater burden of practical care than women who are looking after husbands with dementia.

Marriage has consistently been found by researchers to protect against dementia. Why, then – assuming my findings can be replicated across a much larger sample – might the supposed advantage of having an (able) living spouse increase the risk of Alzheimer's viz-a-viz the other forms of dementia? Why, moreover, should the risk of AD be even higher if the living (able) spouse is female? And why should having had a female spouse disabled by dementia so significantly increase the risk of dementia in her widower?

There was only one divorced person, a woman, in the comparison group but five people in the dementia sample (four women, one man) were divorced. All six divorced people had spent the vast majority of their adult lives without a spouse. Two of the dementia sample had been completely abandoned by their husbands when their children were very young, and two others had themselves been wives who had abandoned their partners and dependent children without notice. The man with dementia whom I have counted as divorced left his wife for another woman, with whom he had a child before their relationship also quickly foundered. Two of the widows in the dementia sample had also been divorced earlier in their lives – one of them being a further example of a young mother abandoned by her husband. One of the married men with dementia had likewise had a previous marriage which ended in divorce (in the wake of a child's death).

Thus, nine of the fifty-nine people in the dementia sample who had ever married had experienced divorce/marital breakdown compared with no-one amongst the fifty-five (of sixty) people in the comparison group who had chosen to marry. (And marital breakdown, as I have already mentioned, is a likely indicator of insecure attachment.)

Widowhood

Current prescriptions for retaining good cognitive function in late life show painfully little regard to the disadvantage most elderly women will have experienced throughout their adult lives. The majority of current nursing home residents, for instance, are from generations where most women lacked the opportunity of an intellectually challenging and fulfilling career, and most lacked the money, time and energy for stimulating activities outside the home. Caring for others was generally their lot, in an era with less labour-saving devices than now, for example far fewer freezers and no supermarket ready-meals.

Women born before the war were expected by society to keep house for their menfolk and children, and to help frail elderly relatives remain in the community. Some wives whose husbands' incomes were sufficient to support the family joined other women who had retired in providing unpaid voluntary services needed by vulnerable members of the community (e.g. by organising and delivering "meals on wheels" for the housebound). Many women, as now, provided daycare for young grandchildren through into their own retirement so that their adult children could work.

Competing domestic responsibilities condemned those from poorer households to low paid and menial jobs, which often involved working unsociable hours and could be physically exhausting. The worst-off could neither afford to leave, nor afford to retire fully when they reached state pension age (Toynbee, 2003).

The usefulness of all these essential but undervalued, demanding, and tradition-ally female activities in keeping people alert and engaged tends to be overlooked by research. Ironically, it took the Second World War to give many of these now elderly women, from whatever background, at least a glimpse of their true occu-pational capabilities. This point is well illustrated in *The Girl from Station X* by Elisa Segrave (2013), in which she describes her privileged mother's (notably tragic) life before the onset of Alzheimer's Disease.

There is now a plethora of official advice about the sorts of activities which older people should pursue in order to stave off dementia, but it can seem to bear little relation to the harsh realities of the lives of the oldest old, and particularly women. I also became very aware as a social worker across the age ranges that the activities outside the home which men and women in their sixties and seven-ties might enjoy and find stimulating were often beyond the energies of those in their eighties.

Many elderly widows, even in the face of increasing physical infirmity, never-theless remain active in mind and body by continuing to carry out the myriad tasks involved in independent living. They clean their homes (generally to a standard envied by their juniors); plan and manage their often frugal incomes; shop fre-quently for groceries, in amounts they can both afford and carry; plan, prepare and cook proper meals; do their own laundry and maybe some ironing; keep in touch with relatives and friends; tend their gardens if they have them; care for, exercise and clean up after any pets; help neighbours frailer than themselves; and also join in whatever social or voluntary activities are accessible to them at their current level of physical ability. Far from being the "couch potatoes" of whom sports scientists and public health gurus despair, most elderly women well earn any time they get to sit down and relax.

This widespread pattern of everyday living amongst elderly widows is patently healthy enough for the vast majority. It can, however, all too easily be disrupted by unresolved mourning, chronic anxiety, depression, and/or incipient dementia – factors which together can conspire to cloud the picture of what really does, and does not, keep dementia at bay.

Health advisors and social planners also tend to assume everyone has personal access to a car with which to get to stimulating pursuits. Away from civic hubs of commercial and academic activity, one only has to pay attention to who is patiently waiting at bus stops or struggling along on foot in all weathers, to rec-ognise the reality that many unsupported women, especially those old enough to have been born before the Second World War, have been getting up and out for exercise (with its likely attendant social engagement) every time they want to go anywhere at all.

Perhaps we should adjust our focus and start asking why it might be that so many solitary, and often care-worn, elderly women are needing to be looked after by someone else for a while before they die.

Conclusions

Dementia, like mental illness, is far more common in subordinate groups in society (e.g. women, people of low socioeconomic status and minority ethnic groups) than in dominant ones (Cochrane, 1983; Horwirtz, 2003).

This situation has also been common in British society for longer than we collectively choose to remember. I am old enough to recall traditional Victorian psychiatric, "subnormality", and geriatric hospitals, whose large, impersonal and sometimes locked, backwards were populated by high numbers of distraught/confused and institutionalised elderly people, most of them women. Wretched lapses into unreality are not as new a phenomenon within British society as we like to believe, although they have rightly become less invisible and therefore harder to ignore.

Women form not only the vast majority of people with dementia (because of their increased susceptibility in oldest old age, as well as because they live longer than men) but they also form the vast majority of unpaid informal carers; the vast majority of very low-paid care employees; and now the vast majority of the high-fee paying care home users.

Meanwhile, institutions which administer to people with dementia tend to be male-dominated, including government and the financial sector which, in the UK, respectively allow and benefit from a lucrative system of for-profit care home provision. The purchase of dementia care at exorbitant and escalating prices is being left to ordinary people and, when they have no private means or when their personal resources run out, cash-strapped local authorities. Dementia is nevertheless presented by government and the media as an enormous current expense to the state/taxpayer. This is disingenuous.

Where is this alleged state expense being incurred?

Funding for dementia research has been lamentably low in the UK relative to that for conditions which present earlier in life and, by contrast, affect at least as many men as women – such as cancer and heart disease.

As for NHS expenditure on dementia care, anyone who has encountered mixed-age NHS wards is likely to have witnessed the widespread failure of our general hospitals to make any adapted provision whatsoever for physically or mentally incapacitated elderly in-patients. Unacceptably low staffing levels in NHS hospitals mean that frail elderly patients tend to be left unfed and sometimes un-toileted as well as completely unstimulated. Even affording inpatient TV/phone, or visitors' car parking at most UK hospitals has, through privatisation, become the preserve of those with above-average means, thus increasing the isolation (and, ironically, thereby impeding the recovery) of the frailest elderly in-patients. This is especially the case in rural areas, where incomes are low and there is little, if any, public transport.

Defensive institutional processes, reinforced by a societal terror of ageing and a pathological obsession with youth, militate against proper investigation into social factors which may have been contributing to high dementia rates in unequal societies such as ours.

Research effort continues to focus on the cascade of intricate biological changes associated with (but not necessarily causing) dementia, or on identifying individual shortcomings which can be blamed for dementia's occurrence. This latter approach demonises the underprivileged whilst allowing the best-resourced in society to feel relatively safe from dementia They feel protected in the knowledge that they had a reasonably good material start in life; had a better than average education; have been equipped to enjoy reading and other intellectual pursuits; have not suffered the impact of a lifetime's physical hardships; have not been mentally derailed by unremitting powerlessness; and can afford to eat well, travel comfortably and benefit from an interesting and stimulating lifestyle.

Dementia particularly baffles us when supposed protective factors such as these mysteriously fail to protect. Perhaps the prevailing paradigm is wrong.

My findings, although they need confirming across much larger, formally controlled samples, suggest that there may be some particularly unfortunate combinations of early and late life experience which can cause people increasingly to withdraw from reality in a desperate bid to survive. The means by which a gradual mental shutdown is achieved is presumably a matter of individual biology.

From my perspective, the origins of dementia, and ways of intercepting it, may be proving elusive because we have yet to contemplate the possibility that psychology could hold the key that will unlock the complex biological puzzle.

References

Bonanno, G. A. (2005). Resilience in the face of loss and potential trauma. *Current Directions in Psychological Science, 14,* 135–138.
Bonanno, G. A. (2009). *The Other Side of Sadness: What the New Science of Bereavement Tells Us about Life After Loss.* New York: Basic Books.
Bowlby, J. (1979). *The Making and Breaking of Affectional Bonds.* London: Tavistock.
Bowlby, J. (1980). *Attachment and Loss, Vol. 3: Loss, Sadness and Depression.* London: Tavistock.
Cochrane, R. (1983). *The Social Creation of Mental Illness.* London: Longmans.
Felitti, V. J., Anda, R. F., Nordenberg, D., Williamson, D. F., Spitz, A. M., Edwards, V., Koss, M. P., & Marks, J. S. (1998). Relationship of Childhood Abuse and Household Dysfunction to Many of the Leading Causes of Death in Adults. The Adverse Childhood Experiences (ACE) Study. *American Journal of Preventive Medicine, 14,* (4): 245–258.
Hofman, A., Rocca, W. A., Brayne, C., Breteler, M. M. B., Clarke, M., Cooper, B., Copeland, J. R. M., Dartigues, J. F., Da Silva Droux, A. Hagnell, O., Heeren, T. J., Engedal,

K., Jonker, C., Undesay, J., Lobo, A., Mann, A. H., Molsa, P. K., Morgan, K., O'Connor, D. W. R., Sulkava, R., Kay, D. W. K., & Amaducci, L. (1991). The Prevalence of Dementia in Europe: A Collaborative Study of 1980–1990 Findings. *International Journal of Epidemiology, 20* (3): 736–748.

Holmes, J. (2017). Roots and Routes to Resilience: Attachment/Psychodynamic Perspectives. *Psychoanalytic Discourse/Discours Psychanalytique (PSYAD), 3*: February. Accessed 20 October 2017.

Horwirtz, A. V. (2003). *Creating Mental Illness*. Chicago: University of Chicago Press.

Moceri, V. M., Kukull, W. A., Emanual, I., van Belle, G., Starr, J. R., Schellenberg, G. D., McCormick, W. C., Bowen, J.D., Teri, T., & Larson, E. B. (2001). Using Census Data and Birth Certificates to Reconstruct the Early-Life Socioeconomic Environment and the Relation to the Development of Alzheimer's Disease. *Epidemiology, 12* (4): 383–389. [Also known as The Epidemiology and Prevention of Dementia (EUROdEm) study.]

Norton, M. C., Østbye, T., Smith, K. R., Munger, R. G., & Tschanz, J. T. (2009). Early parental death and late-life dementia risk: findings from the Cache County Study. *Age and Ageing, 8* (13): 340–343. https://doi.org/10.1093/ageing/afp023 Accessed 20 October 2017.

Persson, G., & Skoog, I. (1996). A prospective population study of psychosocial risk factors for late onset dementia. *International Journal of Geriatric Psychiatry, 11*: 15–22.

Pressman, G. A., & Bonanno, D. L. (2007). With whom do we grieve? Social and cultural determinants of grief processing in the United States and China. *Journal of Social and Personal Relationships, 24*: 729–746.

Segrave, E. (2013). *The Girl from Station X*. London: Union Books.

Toynbee, P. (2003). *Hard Work: Life in Low Pay Britain*. London: Bloomsbury.

Chapter 8

The role of reminiscence groups in the care of people with dementia and their families

Pam Schweitzer

Reminiscence is about exploring with others one's past life, going back over it, sharing important bits of it and listening to other people's memories as a stimulus. It's an important thing to do, especially as you get older and do not have older people around you who you would naturally want to remember with. Setting up groups is a way to enable people to visit their lives, their past lives – but also to bring that past into the present.

Sadly, in the UK there are very few programmes for both the person with dementia and their carer or family member. *Remembering Yesterday Caring Today* (RYCT) provides a way to bring carer and cared for together and use reminiscence and creative arts to explore shared memories. People with dementia and their carers/family members have an opportunity to be social and in public together in a supportive and enjoyable environment. ". . .activities stimulate laughter and fun, the shared activity is both bonding and socialising as well as triggering recognition and stimulating memory through action" (Daniela, 2013, RYCT Apprentice. Personal communication).

Since 1997, the European Reminiscence Network has been developing a reminiscence project in which families who are caring for a relative with dementia at home can participate in a series of reminiscence sessions with professional and volunteer support. The purpose of these sessions is to engage people with dementia and their family carers together in remembering, sharing, recording and celebrating their long lives.

This project, created by the European Reminiscence Network, has been refined and developed over seventeen years. Partners from different European Union countries have worked together to develop an international training and accreditation programme so that we could spread the work in our own countries and ensure that there would be competent group facilitators to lead it in the future.

A manual of best practice from across all European RYCT projects was first published by the European Reminiscence Network in 1999, and translated into six languages (Bruce et al., 1999).

My colleague Errolyn Bruce (Bradford University, UK) and I, together with other EU project partners and consultants, further refined the programme over time, trialing alternate models and gathering extensive evidence. The focus is now on the twelve-week programme model, incorporating three to five separate carers' meetings. By 2007, we had written the twelve-week programme into the publication called *Remembering Yesterday, Caring Today: Reminiscence in Dementia Care*, published in 2008 by Jessica Kingsley (Schweitzer & Bruce, 2008). This is the basis of what we use today. Apprentices we train attend a two-day preparatory training before working with couples attending the weekly reminiscence sessions, and they use this publication to support their practice. Others across the UK who wish to incorporate reminiscence into their work with people with dementia also use this publication as their very practical handbook.

The structure of the twelve weeks is as follows. We hold a series of two-hour sessions following the life course of people with dementia and their carers. We use reminiscence and creative approaches to help everyone express themselves. It is a programme which aims to include the person with dementia *and* their caregiver and therefore impacts upon their relationship, most often in a very positive way.

Couples, namely a person with dementia and a person looking after them, such as a partner, son or daughter or sibling, work together, with both having the opportunity to reminiscence and do creative, enjoyable activities related to recalled experience. An equal role for couples is provided. Once people with dementia are settled – usually by week three of the programme – we introduce a separate carers-only session within the two hours every few weeks.

The purpose of these carers' meetings is to allow carers to reflect on their own responses and the responses of the person they care for to the programme. Carers also may share any concerns, develop peer relationships and learn strategies for enriching daily life at home. While carers meet, their people with dementia continue the themed activities set up during the session. Often sharing back with the couples following these separate meetings can produce surprises and new learning about their loved one. For example, two gentlemen during a London-based programme happily rubbed flour, rolled and cut scones while their wives attended the carers' meeting. Later, as baking smells permeated the room, the wives told us that neither man had ever made scones before!

One carer expressed enormous relief that she and her partner could participate together in a relaxed way as she had been so reassured by the promise that "at no point are you responsible for your person". When you are in a caregiving relationship you often feel exhausted by the constant "monitoring" you feel you have to do to protect the person and others from the impact of their unpredictable behaviour. This can lead to withdrawal and isolation as the couple can feel ashamed or embarrassed when appearing in public.

A recent RYCT programme in Canada, set up by an apprentice, Christine King, also included a research element. Carers/family supporters and people with dementia were invited to reflect on their learning during the programme:

> I was reminded of communication methods I had used in the past and particularly how I could now use them to pull hubby out of his morose moments.

I learned to be more patient with my dad, and ask him questions about his life.

Participants from other countries have said:

> For me this was a powerful experience. It has helped me to think with grati-
> tude about the good life we have lived together. And we still have a good life.
> (Caregiver, Finland)

> It's just great to have shared positive time together. However challenging it
> is, I want to continue talking to [my partner] about our pasts using objects,
> photos, music and so on.
> (Caregiver, London)

> Other people's memories triggered off my own. I need to keep in touch more
> with my old friends to keep my memories alive.
> (Person with dementia, London)

The twelve-week programme follows the life cycle from early beginnings in
which participants share how they were named and what their name might mean.
This immediately brings out the often surprising and wonderful diversity in a
group.

Reminiscence life course themes include:

- Childhood
- Neighbourhood
- Schooldays
- Starting working life
- Going out and looking good
- Courting days
- Marriage and settling down
- The next generation

Optional additional themes have included:

- Grandparents
- War years
- Holidays
- Special celebrations
- Shopping in the past
- Favourite recipes
- Gardening
- Hobbies
- Cinema and entertainment
- Journeys to remember

Each session uses familiar creative reminiscence methods which include:

Handling familiar objects from the past; for example a 92-year-old woman with frailties was presented with a typewriter just like the one she had used as a young office worker. As she started to load the paper and hit the keys quite hard, it was as though her body remembered what to do. She was the only person in the room who knew how to manage the carriage return at the end of each line and make the machine produce its familiar "ting" sound. After the physical action of typing, she was then shown an enlarged photo of people she worked with and was able to recall the names of her colleagues, information which her daughter had never heard before. The typewriter was a bridge enabling the participant to bring past competence into the present and gain self-confidence and recognition. Bringing past and present together enables the person with dementia and the carer to feel a stronger sense of their individual identity over time, at a point when it is most endangered.

Use of photographs; for example, a man with dementia whose wedding photograph had been enlarged, was able to describe his appearance and clothing on the day and his wife's beauty, following up with the spontaneous comment: "And she is still beautiful." Significant photos remind couples of the centrality of their relationship over time. New captions incorporating spontaneously recalled detail can be incorporated into photo albums or scrapbooks. Families are invited to keep a record in the scrapbooks provided of the stories they have recovered during all the sessions, together with the resulting drawings and photos.

Improvised drama; for example, small-group re-enactments of moments remembered, sparked by the theme of childhood, around family mealtimes and associated rituals and exchanges. We often celebrate together the long-term relationships of participants through re-enactment of key family events such as weddings and christenings. Drama activity creates an atmosphere of fun and spontaneity which encourages participation in an environment completely protected from experiences of "failure".

Music and dance; for example, remembering music from "courting days" (like "big band orchestras") and dancing as the music plays, this triggering many more memories of associated people and places. Dance gives hand and eye contact, using familiar rhythms and tunes and remembered steps. People regain a sense of rhythm and movement and enjoy dancing together, often for the first time in many years.

Singing together; for example, remembering popular songs connected with the participants' past and remembering the words collaboratively (through combined effort as no-one could remember them all alone) and sharing events and situations recalled from these times. Singing together promotes a sense of belonging in the group and provides many opportunities for pooling individual memories into a meaningful combination.

Cooking; for example, handling raw ingredients, like uncooked sausages and rehearsing a remembered recipe, peeling potatoes, kneading the ingredients for bread, and mixing butter and flour for pastry. These familiar actions, with associated smells and, ultimately, tastes when they are cooked, enable participants to re-engage with past skills.

Drawing/painting; for example, volunteers and people with dementia sharing memories on a topic (such as "the place where I grew up") and then drawing the remembered place, often in a diagrammatic way or focusing on one detail.

Writing; for example, when a volunteer writes down what a person with dementia has been talking about in a one-to-one exchange, so that what that person says can be heard and valued by the whole group.

Dressing up; for example, when remembering preparing to go out and enjoy themselves in much younger days, wearing important accessories or hair-styles, putting on items which represent things they wore for "glamour".

Memory boxes; for example, working together with a volunteer or family member to create a "life portrait" containing small, but important items of memorabilia, photos, objects, gifts, holiday souvenirs, maps, etc. Working on these memory boxes provides an on-going constructive activity around displaying memories, and this can then be shared with relatives, friends and even a wider public. It is also affirming for couples to have art reflecting their experiences and stories recognised and shared. Artists who co-produce with the person with dementia help imagine and deliver a creative display of the memory box contents. These memory boxes have been used in social situations such as days out with the family where they can be a focus of lively conversation or to smooth the transition from home to care home, so that the person with dementia is introduced to the new environment in a meaningful way. They have also been used at funerals as a means of enabling grandchildren to learn more about their grandparent.

Practical activities; for example, making Christmas decorations or potting up cuttings of plants: activities which are absorbing, but which also trigger memories and conversation on related themes in a relaxed atmosphere.

All the activities need to include the following essential elements:

- Multi-sensory stimulation.
- Non-verbal forms of communication.
- Time to listen well and reflect back what people have said to encourage and support them.
- One-to-one and small group working, as well as work with the whole group.
- Themes of common interest where everyone can contribute stories such as childhood, schooldays, holidays, homes and gardens and animals.
- Exploration of each weekly theme through a variety of approaches and stimuli.
- Plenty of thematically related reminiscence objects to handle.
- A wide range of activities to choose from: drama, music, dance, drawing, painting, writing, cooking, anything in fact, so there are opportunities to try new things in each session.

RYCT Apprenticeships

It is now an important part of running any RYCT programme that it should attract and support apprentices (volunteers in a training role), who will build skills on the project, and build relationships too. They bring their own arts skills into reminiscence work, and they enjoy having fun and being creative with the families and one another. Apprentices attend weekly sessions and write an extended essay about their own learning on the project. They are assessed by expert project leaders and become accredited RYCT facilitators. This scheme is running in many of our partner countries, including Czech Republic, France, Spain and the UK. We are very conscious that we need to build into the project a legacy element so that it can continue into the future. The aim is for the apprentices to become proficient in the RYCT process and go on to deliver the project in their own workplaces or on a freelance basis.

Feedback from participants

Art was used in every session. Music, objects, pictures, drama, drawing . . . This helped people remember more and more vividly, made the memories visible and stimulated conversation and communication.

(Finland)

Creative activity gives a space for individual expression, for communication of immediate feelings in the "here and now". It does not require strict intellectual and logical thinking.

(Slovakia)

Capturing emotions, attitudes, feelings, bringing facts and knowledge to the surface, using emotional memory and expressing the values of the individual person.

(Slovakia)

It is very touching that we can remember our childhood and families.

(Czech Republic)

The family carers discovered old photos, diaries, pictures, documents and other things and how useful these things could be in improving the quality of the care they could give to their relatives.

(Czech Republic)

They felt joy when they discovered that something they had seen working in the group situation of the sessions could also work at home.

(Czech Republic)

Volunteers realised that people with dementia could be active – at least in certain situations – much more active than they had thought.

(Germany)

Volunteers became more creative and more daring in how they interacted with persons with dementia.

(Germany)

I felt great that I have laughed so much with my wife. She doesn't laugh at home anymore.

(Netherlands)

Taking care of my husband has become less burdensome. I am less afraid for the future.

(Netherlands)

It is inspiring, and it is a way to keep memories alive. It is a good way to work together (the carer and the person with dementia). The best way to reminisce is doing things instead of only talking.

(Netherlands)

A typical response by carers to qualitative evaluation was as follows:

I'm sure I speak for a lot of family carers here when I say that we have really appreciated these reminiscence afternoons. I'm a different person completely from when we first started meeting. I was a wreck. Now I feel I've got a lot of friends, everyone's friendly and I can talk to everybody here in the group. It's a great project. A marvellous thing.

(John Pettit)

A comment from a participant with dementia was:

I would like to say how much I have enjoyed meeting you all and thank you for your friendship. I mean all of you, helpers as well. I felt shy at first of mixing with strangers and did not really want to come. But even after the first week I looked forward to the next Tuesday as I felt warm and welcome and we started to talk openly about our experiences. We laughed, talked about old films and sang songs from days gone by. These weeks have brought me out of myself, so I thank you all once again. It has been great.

(Bill Parker)

Here are a few of the comments made by family carers who had participated, comments which are typical of carers' reactions across all projects:

I didn't feel so alone, just knowing that other people were in the same boat.

He was just normal like the rest of them. I do find it a bit embarrassing, sometimes. It was good in the group not to have to keep apologising for him.

Now we have more things to talk about.

We could share something together.

I realised there were things that you could do. I found it helpful to discover an activity I could share with L. Rather than just sitting looking at each other, we could share something together.

"Success story" award

We were delighted that the RYCT project received the honour of this award from the European Commission in 2016.

This is their announcement of the award:

> "Remembering Yesterday, Caring Today Training" has been selected as a "success story" by a panel of experts from the Directorate-General for Education and Culture of the European Commission.
>
> "Success stories" are finalised projects that have distinguished themselves by their impact, contribution to policy-making, innovative results and/or creative approach and can be a source of inspiration for others. The choice of your project as a success story was made on the basis of a selection process according to rigorous criteria regarding the quality, relevance and results of your project.

A conference entitled "Remembering Yesterday, Caring Today" was held at University of Greenwich on 16–18 November 2017 to celebrate and mark the twentieth anniversary of the project. One of the highlights was the presentation by David Woodhead who through the use of an ethnographically informed participant observation research approach presented very encouraging and positive results concerning the efficacy of RYCT for both carers and those that they care for. The research evaluation report entitled "Remembering Yesterday, Caring Today – participants' voices" is available from the author.

It is another example of the centrality of this creative approach acknowledged in the recent report "Creative Health: The Arts for Health and Wellbeing" outlining the outcome of an enquiry by the All-Party Parliamentary Group on Arts, Health and Wellbeing (2017) co-chaired by the Right Honourable Lord Howarth of Newport.

Twenty years on, it is most exciting and gratifying that the contribution of an approach which uses reminiscence and the arts so extensively in a relational context is being acknowledged as essential in the care of those living with dementia and their families.

Appendix

RYCT statistics over four years, 2010–2014

The RYCT training and apprenticeship was developed across Europe through two European Partnership grants.

During this period:

- 500 families joined the project (1,000 individuals)
- 400 reminiscence sessions were held
- 400 people undertook the two-day training course
- 146 RYCT apprentices graduated

Since 2014, the project has continued in partner countries, despite the end of our European funding, and figures are as follows:

- 163 couples joined the project (327 individuals)
- 300 reminiscence sessions were held
- 601 people undertook the two-day training course
- 94 RYCT apprentices graduated

References

All-Party Parliamentary Group on Arts, Health and Wellbeing (2017). *Creative Health: The Arts for Health and Wellbeing.* Inquiry report co-chaired by Rt Hon Lord Howarth of Newport. www.artshealthandwellbeing.org.uk/appg-inquiry/Publications/Creative_Health_Inquiry_Report_2017_-_Second_Edition.pdf. Accessed on 15 December 2017.

Bruce, E., Hodgson, S., & Schweitzer, P. (1999). *Reminiscence with People with Dementia: A Handbook for Carers.* London: European Reminiscence Network.

Schweitzer, P., & Bruce, E. (2008). *Remembering Yesterday, Caring Today – Reminiscence in Dementia Care: A Guide to Good Practice.* London: Jessica Kingsley.

Woodhead, D. L. (2017). *Remembering Yesterday, Caring Today – Participants' Voices.* A research evaluation report presented at the conference entitled "Remembering Yesterday, Caring Today" at University of Greenwich, London on 16–18 November 2017. Web link: www.rememberingtogether.eu/David-Woodhead-report-RYCT.pdf See also: www.rememberingtogether.eu and www.europeanreminiscencenetwork.org

Chapter 9

My sister, disappearing

Hazel Leventhal

In July 2010 the Alzheimer's Society organised a conference entitled "The National Dementia Declaration", which was set up to decide upon future strategy for dealing with people who are diagnosed with dementia. There was no such strategy when I joined the Alzheimer's Society in 2000 shortly after my only sister, Frances, was diagnosed with early-onset Alzheimer's Disease, when she was still in her fifties.

When someone first becomes aware that they are having problems with their memory, or when a close family member alerts them to this fact, there starts a long and often difficult process until they are eventually given a diagnosis. Most of the tests she underwent concentrated on the physiological. There was very little mention of the psychological impact of early relationships, family ties and social isolation and I believe that all these have an important part to play in the possible development of dementia. I accompanied my sister along her journey into Alzheimer's from the very beginning and was her advocate along the way. I had to fight every bureaucratic battle for her once she lost her faculties and I was the witness to every struggle she had in trying to adjust to her new life whilst coping with the erosion of her brain. To watch someone succumbing to Alzheimer's is one of the saddest things one can ever witness so, whilst watching my sister slowly drowning in the lonely sea of forgetting, I did everything within my power to try to help and protect her. Part of that involved exploring her past, seeking some clue as to why she had developed this insidious disease. What emerged seemed profoundly interesting and relevant.

Frances was born in late 1940 into a world at war and I wonder if the present explosion in people being diagnosed with dementia may be due to the traumas they endured during their childhoods in the Second World War. Her father died during that war, leaving her fatherless at the age of 3 months. Our mother went back to live with her mother, who looked after my sister, while mum went back to work full-time to help support her family. Our grandfather, who Frances regarded as a surrogate father, died when my sister was 3 and she was then evacuated to Wales on her own, as our mother had to continue working, and she was taken in by a couple unable to have children of their own. When she returned to London at the end of the war she was sent to boarding school as our mother felt this was the best way for her to be looked after and to meet other children. I can only imagine the sense of abandonment and rejection she must have felt. When Frances was six and a half my mother re-married and I was born when she was nearly 8. It was only then that she returned to "a normal family life". It is my belief that she learned to block or switch off memories at an early age, as they were too painful for her, and also no-one knows what kind of experiences she went through during her years of being evacuated and at boarding school. This catalogue of broken attachments could not have left her unscathed and it is not surprising that she suffered later in life.

As a child I remember my sister being very shy and reserved. Whenever we went out together she was always keen to go home again. Towards the end of her life she often asked me when she was going home, as do so many people with dementia as though they know they have lost their place of safety. She was academically gifted and won a scholarship to a highly-regarded girls' grammar school. She held responsible and interesting jobs as an adult, her final one being the departmental secretary to the Professor of Pharmacology at King's College, a job she held for over twenty-four years. She never seemed to want to sustain a long-term relationship, despite receiving many offers of marriage. The one man I believe she did love, when in her twenties, betrayed her so her trust was once again shattered. She was a loyal and close friend to her girlfriends and enjoyed their company and visiting them until her illness prevented that.

Frances had always been someone it was difficult to get close to physically but when I married and had children, she became very close to them and poured out all her love and affection towards them. She was the perfect auntie who introduced her nephews to the theatre, concerts and art galleries. It was only when she was well into her illness that she became physically affectionate in the last few years of her life. Her relationship with my father was amicable but I do not recall him ever being physically affectionate with her, possibly for fear of that being misunderstood. Looking back I can see that she tried very hard to get my father to love her, which I also think he tried to do, but his attitude towards her was one of responsibility and duty rather than unconditional love. I think he found it well-nigh impossible to give her the kind of love that she craved but, sadly, never received.

My mother clearly did love her and tried to show her that, but their early attachment had been so disrupted that I believe my sister lost her trust in that love and was never able to find it with anyone again. I've been told that she welcomed my birth because it meant she could come back into the family, as she returned from boarding school soon after I was born. I can only recall her being kind and caring and protective throughout my childhood. She was often responsible for me as our mother continued to work full-time from the time I was three months old. Although we had au pair girls they too needed some time off, so she often looked after me at home and would take me with her when visiting her friends. I looked to her for comfort and support when our mother wasn't around, which was often, and this was one of the reasons I wanted to reciprocate and look after her in her time of need. Although very different we had always been close.

It was during our mother's final illness that I became fully aware of how ill my sister was as well. Once when visiting my mother she said to me "Frances isn't right you know." I said "Yes, I know – but don't worry, I'll look after her." It took me some months to persuade her to see a doctor as when I suggested it she said, "Why – just because I'm a bit forgetful?" I said I felt there was more to it and reminded her that she hadn't seen a doctor in eight years and it might be a good idea to have a check-up. Reluctantly she agreed and so we embarked on the first of our many visits to doctors, consultants, neurologists and specialist nurses. She was in her early fifties when her illness began to show but the diagnosis took over two years from GP referral before it was confirmed. I think they were reluctant to diagnose Alzheimer's in one so young. Our mother died before Frances received her diagnosis so she never knew that it was early-onset Alzheimer's but I believe in her heart she did know and it was too unbearable for her.

After our mother died my sister and my elderly father were left living together and somehow they coped as their different capacities complemented each other. However, one evening after a distressed call from my father to tell us that my sister had flooded their bathroom, again, we were driving back from sorting things out when my husband said "They can't go on like this" and I agreed. It was his suggestion that they should come and live with us. When we got home we discussed this with our sons, who were then aged 17 and 19. At the end of this discussion our elder son stood up and said "Well, it's going to be hell but we have to do it." That just about summed up the situation. It took nearly a year to sort out the living arrangements as we had to sell our house and their flat and buy one house where we could all live together. My father was only too glad to relinquish the responsibility and come to live with us but my sister was not happy about moving from the flat where they had lived for thirty-nine years.

When we all started to live together it was during what I call the "transitional" period of Alzheimer's when the person living with it is acutely aware that something is wrong but they don't really know exactly what it is or how to deal with it. Frances was angry, depressed, fearful, anxious and confused. It must have all been so bewildering for her. We were going for regular tests at The National Hospital for Neurology but this was before there were any drugs available to combat some of the symptoms and keep people functioning at a higher level. Aricept and Reminyl were beginning to be considered but at the time the UK's National Institute for Clinical Excellence (NICE) were not allowing them to be prescribed on the NHS. After two years of trying to get her onto some medication that might help she was eventually allowed to take Aricept if we could get a private prescription for it, which we did, and her Consultant at The National said he would still monitor her on the NHS. It did help for about twenty months. Perhaps if she had been allowed to take it earlier she would have been kept at a higher cognitive level for longer.

I tried to allow Frances as much independence as possible but it was very difficult when she could no longer do things such as use a front door key or manage money. Now there are dementia cafes and "Singing for the Brain" groups and a greater awareness of the needs of those with dementia, but these were not on offer then. At home our kitchen had little post-it notes on all the cupboards and drawers saying what was in each one to make things a bit easier for her. However subsequently over time she forgot how to write and then how to read. For someone who had been an avid reader this was such a loss. We tried to include her in pleasurable activities but sometimes these backfired. We once took her to the theatre and she had been looking forward to it. However she sat throughout the performance with her eyes closed and I realised that it was all too overwhelming for her so we stuck to less stimulating outings such as garden centres or parks. Even those became bewildering for her though, as I recall, walking round a garden centre which she seemed to be enjoying when she suddenly looked at me with fear in her eyes and said "Hazel, I don't know how to get home from here." I reassured her that we would be taking her home and there was no need to worry but I could see the terror that threatened to engulf her at any moment. How must it be to live with that kind of fear each and every day?

As time went on she became ever more childlike and dependent. She only seemed to feel safe if she could see me so would follow me everywhere, hovering at my shoulder. It was like living with a toddler who needs to keep you in sight all the time except that with a toddler they become a bit more independent and resilient with each day that passes. With Alzheimer's it is the other way round and each day is an almost imperceptible slipping back into a more dependant state. I have the utmost respect and admiration for people who look after their loved ones on their own. I was lucky enough to have a loving and supportive husband and two sons to help me.

At the beginning some family members said we weren't being fair on our sons by forcing them to live with someone with Alzheimer's but, looking back, I feel they acquired a depth of patience, tolerance and compassion that otherwise they may not have achieved for many years. They also had a different take on many things. For instance, they offered to look after her between them on some weekends to allow us some time off and they would take it in turns to go out. After one such weekend we returned home and I asked how it had all gone. Our elder son said a friend had invited him to go and play snooker on the Saturday evening, when he was looking after auntie. I said "Oh, I am sorry – what did you do? Have a takeaway pizza and watch a movie?" and he said "No, I played snooker." "Oh," I said "but what about auntie?" "I took her with us," he replied. Such a simple solution and one she enjoyed but somehow I wouldn't have thought of it.

There were many occasions when humour saved the day but it is rather easy to lose one's sense of humour when living with a disease like Alzheimer's. It not only robs someone of their cognitive abilities and their memories but sometimes also of their joie de vivre. However I was helped by my husband's and our sons' ability to see the funny side of things and even Frances could be cajoled into laughter at times. There was also a much darker side though, particularly one dreadful day when she asked me to kill her because she said she no longer felt like a person and wanted an end to it all. I was able to sit down with her and cuddle her and explain that some people get horrible illnesses like cancer or multiple sclerosis or motor neurone disease but that she was not alone and we would be with her and help her. I was left devastated and in tears by this conversation but as my husband pointed out to me a short while later she had forgotten all about it and was able to carry on with the day as though the conversation had never taken place.

Soon after coming to live with us I knew it was not good for Frances to be stuck at home all day with just my father so with the help of Jewish Care I arranged for her to go to a day care centre. We went to have a look at it first and she turned to me and said "I can't come here, Hazel, it's full of old people." The lady showing us round quickly said "Yes, you see how many people we have here Frances and I so need someone to help out." "Oh," Frances said "You mean you want me to help you with looking after everyone?" and she said "Yes" so that was the basis on which she agreed to go and she did try to help in little ways such as laying the table at mealtimes and chatting to the other people there and joining in the games they played. After about eighteen months though, her condition had deteriorated and the day care centre said that her behaviour was too challenging. They then went on to say that they could no longer have her there.

Things had also become more difficult at home and our social worker said the time had come for Frances to move into residential care as it was just too difficult and dangerous for her to continue living with us. Some of our family found this decision extremely difficult to understand as they had never fully appreciated the extent of her illness, mainly because whenever they saw her she seemed to be reasonably OK, chatting and smiling and appearing much as she had always been. They didn't see the difficulties that she had with everyday activities and the amount of work that went on behind the scenes. One of my cousins even said to me "You could go on looking after her for another year or so." Frances had been living with us for three and a half years at that point and needed almost twenty-four-hour care. Once she fell down the stairs but luckily only sustained a broken toe. Sometimes she would come into our room in the middle of the night expecting to be taken somewhere or she would walk round the house with nothing on. Occasionally she would lose her temper and break things or run out of the front door and down the street and I'd have to go after her as she could so easily have run into the road. I had bought a medic alert bracelet for her soon after she started living with us, which proved very useful as at the beginning she used to go for walks but would sometimes get lost and finish up at the police station.

Once Frances started living in a home I visited her every week and although the staff were kind and caring, the first few weeks were harrowing. Each week she would ask me when she was coming home until eventually I had to say that this was where she was living now and wouldn't be coming back to live with us. She took this very badly and began screaming and banging her head on the table. One of the staff came and helped to calm her down and another one brought her a cup of tea and a piece of cake. I left that day in tears but looked back to see her calmly eating her cake apparently perfectly contented.

After living in this home for about eighteen months they too decided that Frances' behaviour was "too challenging" for her to stay as she was disrupting other residents. Sometimes she would run down the corridors and the staff were unable to catch her and occasionally she would take hold of another resident's hand and get them to run with her. I can imagine it was very distressing for all concerned and some relatives of residents had complained. We had to find another home for her. This proved difficult but eventually it was achieved and she seemed more settled in a smaller place with a lovely garden. I visited every week and was often in phone contact as well.

One morning I had a call from the home to say that Frances had fallen out of bed. They were sending her to the Royal Free Hospital in Hampstead to be checked over as she seemed to be in pain when she stood up. I went there and spoke to the Ward Sister to explain more about Frances to the staff. Unfortunately she had shattered her hip and needed a hip replacement. The doctor I saw said that unless an emergency came in he would operate on her in the morning. I asked if he did not consider this to be an emergency and after I said that I knew the National Guidelines stated that someone who has a shattered hip should be operated on within twenty four hours, he agreed that he would operate. After the operation Frances had no recollection of her fall and was not aware of having had an operation so tried to walk immediately. Unlike most people who've had hip replacements, who are naturally somewhat wary of walking at first, she had no such inhibitions and the staff had to be careful that she wasn't walking too much. She healed well and they sent her back to the home sooner than they would have done as they felt she would receive better care there than in hospital. I understand they now have a Leader in Dementia Care at this hospital who is responsible for accompanying dementia patients at their appointments and ensuring that things run smoothly. That is progress indeed and I hope it spreads to other hospitals.

Alzheimer's eventually affects every action that we perform so Frances gradually lost the ability to do everything and I had to watch her forget how to walk, how to stand up and sit down by herself, how to eat on her own and, finally, how to swallow – which inevitably led to her death. When she could no longer remember how to swallow, the home asked me if I wanted her to be tube-fed and after much thought I decided it would be kinder not to put her through the trauma of being taken to hospital and fitted with a feeding tube as she had no quality of life and tube-feeding would just prolong her suffering. Maybe some people would disagree but I felt it was more humane to let her go. She had been suffering from Alzheimer's for about fifteen years and to prolong her life for a few more days, or even weeks, seemed to me to be cruel.

I have shared these reminiscences about my sister because I feel that her early childhood goes a long way to explaining her complicated relationship with her own memory. Our memories are fundamental to who we are and when we lose them then we are nothing; lost and floundering in a bewildering world as we can see in Josh Appignanesi's film. The world became a totally lonely, confusing and frightening place for my sister, as I suspect it does for all Alzheimer's patients. If she had been given the chance to talk to someone skilled in listening then perhaps some of that fear would have lessened and she would have been able to share some of her inner world with someone she felt could understand her. The very end of Alzheimer's is an unreachable place that no-one else can really enter. The only things that seem to be able to penetrate it are music, smell and touch. Until people are no longer able to communicate at all then the means to help them communicate should be available.

It is now up to psychotherapists to make themselves available and to make their services known to people with dementia and their carers. Possibly more psychotherapists will feel able to offer help to carers. My view is that there is a truly valuable opportunity in working with patients with dementia and that if therapists can pool and share some of their acquired knowledge of the backgrounds, childhood experiences and feelings of people who have developed dementia, then this could prove to be a useful research tool as well as providing solace to those living with this illness. The more we know about the background environment of those who live with dementia, the more light may be shed on who is most likely to develop this disease. Dementia is a disease of the brain and therefore a huge territory that is largely unmapped. Working with those who have dementia, and the people who look after them, gives us an opportunity to journey into this little-known country. We are *all* at risk of developing dementia so the sooner we have some maps to help us find our way around this largely unexplored terrain, the better.

Chapter 10

Therapeutic work with people with dementia using an attachment, psychoanalytic and person-centred approach

The Talking Therapies Project, a Department of Health and Age UK initiative

Anastasia Patrikiou

The purpose of this chapter is to present therapeutic work carried out within a counselling service I was engaged to establish and manage for Age UK Camden (previously, Age Concern Camden), the aim of which was to provide therapy for older people with early to mid-stage dementia and for older people from Black and Minority Ethnic groups. The focus of this particular chapter is on the therapeutic work we did with people with dementia. Through the presentation of clinical material I hope to illustrate how therapeutic work with people with dementia impacted on the users and also impacted on and challenged the therapists.

In 2006, following a bid process, Age UK Camden took part in one of twenty-nine national pilot programmes funded by the Department of Health under the Partnerships for Older People Projects (POPP) initiative. POPP's objective was to improve the quality of life of older people through a focus on a healthier lifestyle and improved wellbeing. In order to foster independent living for as long as possible, it aimed to increase the number and quality of preventative services. The projects ranged from services such as lunch clubs, to more formal preventative initiatives in secondary and tertiary care (Windle et al., 2009). One important area of focus was dementia and Alzheimer's disease in particular.

Statistics provided by the Alzheimer's Society show that 225,000 people develop dementia every year with the numbers projected to reach 1,000,000 by 2021. Sixty thousand deaths every year are attributed to dementia. The financial cost of dementia comes to £26 billion per year. Carers save the country £11 billion per year (Alzheimer's Society, 2016).

Delaying the progression of dementia is possible primarily through early diagnosis, medical support and related services, but also through an improved quality of life which includes therapeutic work. According to the Executive Summary of the National Evaluation of POPP (Windle et al., 2009), the Department of Health was ultimately successful in achieving this aim through implementing an holistic approach to the problem.

The Talking Therapies Project was set up within the generic Counselling Service for Older People established nine years earlier by Age UK Camden. For a while the Counselling Service was the only such service specifically dedicated to this particular group and to date continues to be one of the very few.

It is indeed astonishing that to this day Age UK Camden still remains one of the very few, if not the only organisation offering a dedicated counselling service to older people. David Richards, psychotherapist, creator and manager of the Counselling Service for many years explains this absence as the result of the uncomfortable feelings older age evokes in our society which he likens to feelings underpinning racism and homophobia. He notes:

> As with other areas of cultural tension, such as racism, both ageism and homophobia can be seen as attitudes that contain powerful feelings beneath the surface of hatred. For individuals and society as a whole, such feelings can also be seen as expressions of what we fear or resist within ourselves.

He believes that "this is the reason why counselling and psychotherapy with older adults has tended to remain in the shadows" (Richards, 2011, p.11).

It is true that our society averts its gaze from later life. This life-stage is airbrushed out of the public discourse and popular culture. The body is wished and pressurised to be an eternal carrier of material youth and a vehicle for on-going consumerism. Vulnerability and need are shunned, shamed and attacked together with those who embody it. Older people stop being considered as a value-creating and enriching part of our society and are instead relegated to the peripheral shadows as invisible burdens to be managed.

Our initial exercise mapping-out what types of services were available for people with dementia in the Borough of Camden indicated that there was very little in terms of longer-term therapeutic support for clients with dementia, either at the stage of diagnosis or thereafter. Medical care needs were met by GPs, mental health care teams for older people and memory clinics. Social care needs were met through care packages provided by Social Services in collaboration with the medical teams, and social needs were met by community centres (many of which have now closed due to cuts, depriving many older people of vital social interaction, activities, learning and communal meals) and organisations such as the Alzheimer's Society as well as Age UK. Therapeutic support was conspicuously absent on this map, which Talking Therapies sought to address.

Implementation

The Talking Therapies Service was set up along the same organisational principles as Age UK Camden's Counselling Service and that of many other services in the voluntary and public sectors, which employ a minimal number of paid managerial and supervisory staff who manage a group of volunteer trainee or qualified counsellors and psychotherapists.

The work was carried out by ten to fifteen volunteers who met with three or four clients each week collectively providing thirty to fifty client hours per week. Volunteers received specialised training in understanding dementia which included appreciating the biological and social aspects of the disease as well as the specificities of working with people with cognitive impairment in the latter part of their lives.

It was important to think about what type of psychotherapeutic service would be beneficial to people with dementia, at which stage and for how long. This had to be balanced with funding considerations and evidence that our work was having a positive impact on the individual.

From an attachment and person-centred psychotherapeutic perspective it is considered possible to work with anyone, no matter how verbally and cognitively disabled they may be. We saw with some of our clients with more severe impairments that the mere presence of a receptive, attentive and attuned individual had a beneficial impact on the client's wellbeing.

Given that this was a novel programme, it was important to *prove* within the budget's constraints, that our service was able to contribute to the wellbeing of our clients and to their ability to remain independent for longer. For this reason it was decided that therapy would be offered to people with early to mid-stage dementia where cognitive capacities are substantial and wellbeing can still be "measured", whether by using assessment tools or reports from our clients, carers and other professionals. Furthermore, it is often at this point in the development of the illness that diagnosis is given and therefore the presence of therapeutic support is crucial to help manage it.

It was also our belief that the internalisation of a positive relational experience was crucial at a moment when everything familiar changes dramatically; when one has a sense of becoming invisible, but reliant and burdensome; where any sense of trust is severely challenged. We thought that it could lead to improved wellbeing and perhaps a better resourced inner world with which to face the oncoming deterioration.

Relevant therapeutic approaches

The three therapeutic approaches which underpinned the thinking in designing the project were attachment theory, psychodynamic theory and the person- centred approach.

Attachment theory provided us with an in depth understanding of the trauma of loss throughout the life cycle, particularly of early loss and its consequences in later life. Attachment theory posits that the presence of an internal secure base is paramount to wellbeing. This is internalised through a nurturing and attuned relationship. The potential, therefore to develop or enhance a secure base at any point in life is ever-present, particularly within the context of a therapeutic relationship. In the case of dementia patients the presence of a therapist trained to provide regularity, attunement and containment, effected changes in how our clients thought, felt and managed their lives.

On the other hand a psychoanalytic understanding helped us understand the links between the terrors of early life and how they may be manifesting in later life and with dementia in particular (Waddell, 2007). As with old attachment patterns, it is important to recognise how early difficulties in facing depressive feelings will determine the ways each individual will respond to the illness.

Psychoanalytic thinking, together with intuition and attunement are helpful in making sense of often incomprehensible, bizarre behaviour in such patients. Feelings are frequently expressed in symbolic acts or thoughts, where metaphor and association are important ways with which to understand them and perhaps verbalise them back to the client. These interpretations may result in great relief and the resolution of relational impasses in the therapeutic relationship.

The concept of projective identification is crucial in this work. With verbal communication failing and psychological functioning happening at early levels of development, projective identification is one important way in which the client communicates with the therapist. Powerful feelings evoked in the therapist are not only an invaluable source of information about the client. They must be worked through in order to enable the therapist to endure the challenges this difficult but rewarding work presents and to protect the client from the therapist's potential for retaliation (Waddell, 2007).

The person-centred approach provided us with the practical tools but also the concepts with which to conduct this work. After all, Tom Kitwood, the social psychologist and psychogerontologist who revolutionised ideas around dementia care, based his person-centred care model for dementia on Carl Rogers' person-centred theories (Kitwood, 1997). It is an approach which unequivocally puts the *person* at the *centre* of care and in which the clinician is interested to know and understand the client's experience. A training in this approach is very well suited to working with this client group.

Volunteers were trained with the following principles in mind:

- To accept the client unconditionally
- To meet the client within her experience and to see the world from the client's perspective
- To understand that everything the client is communicating is important, even if it is repeated
- To believe the narrative as true to the client's experience
- To affirm the sense of personhood that the client is conveying through the narrative
- To accept that there are no targets and aims for the client
- To be as genuine as possible
- To be able to hold and metabolize the client's distress
- To be vigilant of one's own reactions and inner processes
- To provide a positive experience of the therapeutic relationship

Case examples

> [The problem] is not simply that of damaged brain cells, but also of the damage to the psychological self and the good feeling that would sustain it. It is, I believe, quite correct to regard unattended dementia as a semi-psychotic state. . . Dementia is envisaged as a break in cohesive awareness, a failure of the process of consistent symbolisation, so that the person has lost his or her bearing in the world, and is invaded by feelings from within. . ... Organic deterioration may induce the breaking down of the individual's life-long defences that leaves the person exposed and vulnerable to catastrophic anxiety and rage. . .
>
> (Kitwood, 1990, p. 49)

It is within this physical, mental and emotional context that we as therapists are invited to work. In the following three case studies I hope to illustrate the effect of the work from three different vantage points. To preserve confidentiality clients' details have been anonymised. It has been difficult to get a personal account from a client, so we gathered evidence from what they communicated in the sessions, the ways in which the therapeutic relationships developed and their responses, and the changes that we saw taking place in their lives. The first case study focuses on the impact of the therapeutic work on the client. The second case study will look at the experience of the therapist in a little more detail. The third case study presents the effect of the service as viewed by another professional service involved in the client's care.

Case 1: Mrs G

When I met up with Mrs G, for an assessment, in the care home where she lived, I deliberated on whether we should offer her the service. Her communication was limited, her sentences trailed off, there were many silences as if lost at what to say, there was some repetition, and her voice was almost inaudible, hampered by Parkinson's disease. Mrs G was an 86-year-old widow with no children. Her much younger sister lived in another country. She appeared to be totally alone. The staff knew nothing about her except for medical and social care information given to them. Living on her own had become unsustainable so she had been transferred to the care home a year earlier. She was in a wheelchair and completely dependent on others for her mobility. She had a history of falls.

Four themes emerged in our initial session: a) her wheelchair was not strong enough to hold her, b) repeated references to "them" who "would throw her out on the street, and take her money", c) death, d) her yearning to see her sister but also her desire not to burden her with her problems.

We decided to offer Mrs G a place on the Talking Therapies Project despite her limited verbal capacity.

Mrs G's preoccupation with the "unsafe chair" was an example of this symbolic representation mentioned earlier and we felt it was a clear communication about an inner state of affairs. Danuta Lipinska in her book *Person-Centred Counselling for People with Dementia* encapsulates the bewilderment of the person with dementia, particularly in the early stages, with three philosophical questions: "Who am I?", "Why am I here?" "Where am I going?" (Lipinska, 2009, p. 24).

In her initial sessions with her counsellor, much of the time was spent talking about the chair and she described her fears that she would "fall through this chair and be a heap on the floor". Mrs G was enabled to address this issue with the manager who did order a new chair for her. The old chair seemed to be fairly sturdy but worn. Mrs G expressed, through the chair, her deep anxiety for her physical and mental safety and the precariousness of the sense of her core self, as overwhelming changes were taking place externally and internally. The loss of her ability to function and keep herself safe we felt was represented by an object which she depended upon but which could actually fail her, perhaps just like she felt she had failed herself. Furthermore Mrs G was utterly alone in the world and whilst her needs were catered for, she was treated rather mindlessly. A sense of a secure base is constructed from a web of human relationships, which in her case, was absent.

A trusting bond was developing between Mrs G and her counsellor. Increasingly she spoke less of the chair, to the extent that it was hardly mentioned some months into the work. It was felt that the safe, consistent, engaging and holding structure of the therapeutic relationship was beginning to fulfil some of her needs for containment, support and safety. The new chair was welcomed when it arrived, but interestingly had become a side-issue in the client's narrative by that point.

Strong feelings persisted around money, an important yardstick of our security. She spoke about how "they" take her money "and want to see her at rock bottom". The counsellor explored with her who "they" may be. It emerged that "they" referred to all those invisible people – the attorney, the accountant – who had been given rights to manage her affairs and about whom she suspected evil intent. Moreover, we know that one of the defences that people with dementia develop as a protection is to blame others for the disintegrating self. It is too painful to own the loss of one's ability, agency and self (Waddell, 2007).

Further exploration of her anxiety and the realities associated with it allowed the client to feel that there may be some part of her life, over which she could have some control. The client and the counsellor discussed how perhaps she could meet the accountant for him to inform her about the state of her finances. Week after week she postponed her decision to request a meeting with him but upon the counsellor's return from a two-week break Mrs G offered her counsellor a gift: she announced excitedly that she had finally asked for the meeting to be arranged. She was very proud of her achievement and somewhat surprised. "You'd be proud of me when I tell you what I've done this week. . . Not bad is it?" The periods of silence had lessened, and she became more articulate and fluent and alive with emotion. It was becoming evident that Mrs G was in fact in the early stages of her illness and her initial lack of verbal communication was more about neglect than a lack of capacity.

Mrs G valued her contact with her counsellor. Between sessions she thought of what she would like to speak about in her next session. When the counsellor was away, Mrs G held onto a piece of paper with the date of their next meeting. In the sessions she was able to explore her frustrations regarding her loss of memory: "Nobody wants this condition that I've got, but that's how it is. Sometimes I forget the words I want to say."

She spoke of her depression too. During one session it suddenly became very dark outside and heavy rain followed. She said: "This is quite how I sometimes feel inside. Sudden dark clouds descend on me and a feeling of torrential rain overwhelms me".

She began laughing occasionally and shared a joke. There were physical signs of change, such as in her posture, for she stooped a lot less. She began speaking more openly about the past.

Mrs G said she had never had therapy before and was initially lost and bewildered regarding the visits of yet another person and revealed that she had viewed the counsellor with suspicion. However, possibly more than most of our clients, Mrs G grasped the purpose of these visits. She verbalised her appreciation one day:

Mrs G: You are the only person I have spoken to about dying, you just don't. . ..
C: It seems important to you to be able to share your concerns and anxieties about it.
Mrs G: Yes. We all have to go at some point I know, but sometimes you wonder how. I don't speak of it to anyone.
C: Though it seems important for you to be able to speak of it.
Mrs G: That's why I'm glad you come to see me. I can have a moan and get things off my chest (laughter).

Case 2: Mrs A

Mrs A was in the early stages of the illness, more physically able than Mrs G, but with greater cognitive impairment. The therapist watched the client's cognitive abilities diminish over the contract period of thirty-four sessions. It will hopefully give us an idea of the difficulties therapists face in this kind of work.

Mrs A was an 80-year-old widow. She had been widowed early on in her life and had a daughter who was very close to her who was attentive and caring. She lived on her own and was quite independent and mobile. The first part of the work took place at Age UK Camden's premises. As her cognitive abilities worsened she was seen at home. Mrs A had just been given a diagnosis of dementia by the Memory Clinic. She was extremely anxious, and already in the first session a pattern of what preoccupied her was clear.

Having never experienced therapy before she had no idea what this was for. It became evident in time that she had learnt early on in life not to talk about herself and to be tough. This was not unusual in this age group. However, whereas in the counselling service most users were actively seeking therapy, in the Talking Therapies Project most users, like Mrs A, were *given* a service, which in time some grew to value. This presented the therapists with a particular set of potential problems.

The absence of choice to attend therapy unsettled some therapists, who struggled with the client's bewilderment at what they were both doing there. In this case Mrs A persisted in asking: "So what do you advise me to do?" The counsellor struggled with the idea that in order to normalise the relationship, "a chat" was appropriate in this case and felt that he was failing at his task to help the client bring material to the session. He often wondered if the client was "unsuitable for therapy".

The therapist was anxious not only because he found himself in the unchartered waters of offering therapy to a person with diminishing cognitive capacities, but also because he was asked to contain the client's extreme levels of anxiety which were being communicated to him viscerally, evoking very powerful reactions.

A recurring theme in the work was the client's preoccupation with plants and their symbolic value of being objects of attention, care or neglect. In the first session she commented on a plant in the therapy room which was in a rather poor condition and she wished to tend and look after it. Further on, and once at home, plants and flowers became companions which the client used to communicate much of what was taking place inside her.

A few sessions into the work, the client was able to reminisce for the first time about the past. She told stories of the war and her life in London, where she had moved at the age of 13, on her own. Then her family followed. She complimented the therapist at the end of that session and said that she had enjoyed talking about herself and remembering the past.

By the fourth meeting, sessions were taking place in the client's flat because she had started finding it difficult to travel. She was more comfortable at home, and some of the anxiety relating to the commute, which had become difficult, had lessened. She described in detail how she raised her daughter, what she had taught her, and wanted reassurance from the therapist that she had done a good job. Her narrative had started becoming increasingly confused. The therapist began to feel more relieved that "material" was being brought to the session and the client had settled somewhat into the flow of what happened in the sessions.

An indication of this emerged when the counsellor's holiday break came up. The counsellor found it extremely hard to announce his leave. He said that he found the sense of abandonment he would cause so painful that he presented himself with excuses postponing telling her, such as, "part of me felt that she would not understand anyway".

When he did announce his leave he saw that he was correct in his assumption that this would be painful for her. She had understood perfectly well, was quite angry, saying that she did not know if she would be around at the end of the therapist's break and that she would call to make an appointment if needed.

The break was useful and essential for the therapist who felt that it had helped lessen his anxiety and he felt freer to engage. He commented:

> I felt I worried less about doing "proper therapy". I asked her a lot more questions, took charge and steered the conversation most of the time, to which she responded well. She spoke about coming to London at thirteen without her mother. She said her mother gave her the enabling tools to be independent. Dad was a professional and very quiet, but tough and he taught her to "speak properly". She grew up in a tough part of the country and spoke of the bravery and ferociousness of her ancestors. She said she had some of this ferociousness coursing in her blood and had survived many difficulties. All these associations of strength, bravery, toughness and ferocity were repeated over and over in the stories she told the counsellor, as she tried to locate within her some sources of strength, to counter her vulnerability and dependence.

But the counsellor was also anxious about his vulnerability and the complexity around the ultimate separation. He wrote: "Felt that we were connected today, but. . . were we merging?" He was not wrong in identifying in the relationship, perhaps indicating a return to very early ways of connecting.

The effects of the illness began manifesting more strongly in the client. The counsellor noted:

> Mrs A was very tired. She seemed to drop off a couple of times. I felt very tired too. She said to me, "You look more tired than I feel!" It was very difficult being with her. She seemed to just stare at me. Much of the time I did not know where her mind was at. She said she was worried about her memory. She didn't know whether she did not want to remember things, or whether she was just losing her memory . . . She was meant to have gone out somewhere that morning but didn't. It felt very difficult. She was worried she would get lost. She again repeated that she liked the sessions because she could ask questions and feel relaxed.

Silences began to grow in the sessions and the therapist's concerns about what therapy "should be" returned. He wrote: "I thought again today that therapy was not suitable for this client. She responds best if I am more chatty and ask more questions, however periods of silence are growing." The client felt his discomfort and said that she felt okay about the quiet moments. He continues: "I find it very unsettling when she is quiet. She seems to stare at me with an enquiring look." It is as if she is desperately trying to find the person within the therapist and through him to be reassured that the person inside her still exists.

Many of her stories were about repair, fixing, making good – as was also the case with Mrs G. She spoke about her calls to the complaints department when younger. Mother taught her how to darn things. Wrote letters of apology to unhappy customers in the company where she had worked. Ran an appliances repair service in the store. Taught her daughter to care for others.

In one session the client said that the clouds were not moving. The therapist thought she seemed particularly vulnerable and frail that day and whilst he felt very connected to her, he felt incredibly emotional and messy. "A couple of times I had to suppress the tears." Regular Sunday meals had stopped with her best girlfriend who had to look after her brother. The counsellor wondered if the client should move into a nursing home soon because it seemed that she was unable to cope with the flat.

Mrs A began to be more and more distracted, preoccupied and repetitive. The counsellor commented: "At times I felt like I just wanted to go home. I couldn't handle it, found it hard to listen to the same things over and over again. I felt bored. Couldn't bear to hear it all again."

The quiet periods became longer and longer. This following session marked a turning point in the work. Mrs A was sinking into her illness. It felt unbearable for both. He noted: "'You seem very quiet'. She said, 'You too!' I took that as a bit of an attack." She then asked him to leave. "When I left the session I felt agitated, unappreciated and angry. The anger stayed with me throughout the day."

Over the next few sessions the quality of silence changed.

> She was very sleepy and spent a large part of the session sitting with eyes closed. She seemed to be resting and breathed out deeply, every now and then. I had a feeling that she enjoyed having someone there watching her sleep, almost like a child. I felt an urge to hold her and let her sleep like a baby.

Mrs A had won in her battle to convey what she needed, which was to be connected to deeply and be held. The therapist, despite his inner struggles and defences, had with his presence encouraged her to do this.

Quiet times seemed comforting now. The counsellor decided he wanted to track Mrs A's gaze in the room. So he followed Mrs A's gaze around the room, looking at the objects behind him, and around him and immersed himself in the present moment. As he did this, the client started talking about what she was thinking.

> Attaching to visual objects, brought stories to the fore. They were often the same stories. I had previously dismissed some of her stories as fabrication and not engaged with them fully, but have been discovering it made a difference if I related to every story she told me as if it were true. I don't think it matters whether something is true or not. It has great significance for her and she wishes to communicate it. I do get very confused from time to time because she mixes up present and past, stories are told with different details. I get a sense of the confusion that reigns within.

It is through stories that we tell that we take ownership of our existence (Lipinska, 2009). Stories are our identity. It is a way of making ourselves known to the other and to ourselves, in fact more persistently if we are losing ourselves. We need the continuity in the story to confirm and re-confirm that we are the masters of our lives. As therapists, a key task is to validate the story. In validating the experience of the story, we validate the self.

> Again she spent most of the session with eyes closed. Opened them and asked me what I was thinking. I felt calm and at peace and did not try to work hard, but tried to tune in to where she was. She seemed to rely on me being there, but did not want to talk at all.

At the next session the counsellor arrived and rang the bell a few times but there was no answer. This was the first time she showed signs of having trouble dealing with the intercom system. Eventually, somehow, he got in and went upstairs. She seemed pleased and had arranged, as she often did, the chairs directly opposite each other. "It was one of the quiet times, when she had her eyes closed. But I was feeling bored and wanted the session to end."

On one occasion the counsellor arrived for his session with Mrs A and bumped into Mrs A's daughter outside the front door. She expressed to him her wish to speak to the manager at Age UK Camden about the fact that her mother was increasingly struggling to cope. They had an appointment at the Memory Clinic the following week and she had to cancel a very important work trip. The counsellor felt uncomfortable that this conversation was taking place outside Mrs A's front door fearing that Mrs A was listening and would feel compromised and betrayed.

He was right. She was waiting for him just inside the door and as he walked in she anxiously and forcefully thrust a note in his hand. It said: "I am anxious and most of the time I am miserable and feel like crying. Sometimes I say to myself 'I am living too long'." With this desperate action she expressed her anguish, her helplessness but perhaps also through writing she ensured that she conveyed all that her illness prevented her from articulating in speech. Furthermore, she indicated how much she had grown to trust him.

She was angry in the session and said that her daughter "had no sympathy". She didn't understand that she was not coping, that she wanted support and companionship. She felt lonely and spent most of the time on her own. The counsellor felt close to tears throughout the session. Mrs A said that she wanted to move into a home, but that her daughter disagreed and apparently told her to "pull herself together". The therapist continues:

> I felt that I wanted to hold her hand and to comfort her. She seemed in such an unforgiving place. She thanked me many times for coming and repeated how much she valued it. She said that she has always put up a courageous front, but that she could not do it anymore.

In the next session Mrs A did not answer the door again despite many attempts. When the therapist got upstairs, she struggled to open the door. Her daughter had to talk her through the motions over the phone. "We sat and I asked what she would like to do. She said she wanted to close her eyes." She had spent a few days at her sister's but had to return because the room was needed there. She sounded disappointed. Today's utter confusion may have had something to do with the pain of this return.

> She showed me her Strelitzia in bloom. . . Nature again. . . She seemed much more like a child and asked for various things: a tissue, a drink. Then she had something stuck in her teeth and asked for a toothpick which she used. At the end of the session she asked what she should do with the toothpick. I was concerned about her wellbeing and reported this to the organisation.

Ten sessions before the end the counsellor informed Mrs A of the date they would be ending. She seemed dazed but peaceful. Most of the session was spent with her eyes closed.

> I watched her like a mother would watch her child. At some point I got distracted by a mark on my hand – she opened her eyes and said I could go if I wanted to. . . I kept on falling into this trap thinking that she wasn't aware of me, or didn't care, but this was not the case. She kept on reminding me of how important my presence was to her.

Mrs G told the counsellor that he understood her even when she was not always "with it". He was kind and he listened to her. The counsellor felt very sorrowful as he witnessed her increasing dependence and the impending ending of their relationship. She slept soundly for most of the sessions. She said that she felt bereft about the ending of the sessions. She liked having him around but preferred not to talk. Spoke about the poppies on the table again. "They had lasted so long." They were company and comforting to her.

Of the penultimate session, the counsellor says:

> She looked beautiful and radiant today. She had taken care over her appearance. Said she felt dazed and muddled. She was concerned that this was the last session. She wanted to sit with her eyes closed. A couple of times I noticed through the reflection of her glasses that she was looking at me lovingly, with a smile in her eyes.

During the last session she was chattier than normal. Mrs A appeared to have thought through her ending and was preparing for life without the sessions. She said that she would miss him and wondered what she would do on Fridays. She said that her daughter was a good girl and stayed with her most days. It was good to have the counsellor around, but she was fine as she was, as well. She liked spending time on her own. Finally she asked him again what *he* would be doing on Fridays.

Case 3: Mr F

In terms of feedback on the efficacy of the work by a third party, I am including a brief outline of the case of Mr F who was reviewed by the Head of the

Dementia Advocacy Service, Age UK before and after the end of the sessions we provided.

Dementia advocates had been asked to meet with Mr F, who was struggling to communicate with close family members regarding his care after diagnosis. Mr F experienced family members as patronising, pushy and disempowering and they found him obstructive and uncollaborative. He was living alone in the house he shared with his wife of many years who had died two years earlier. He suffered deeply from this loss. When the advocates met him for the first time he was extremely anxious and angry, but also resigned. He was offered a basic care package, as he was still fairly self-sufficient and was referred to the Talking Therapies Project to be assessed for counselling.

In my initial counselling assessment visit, Mr F took me on a tour of his home which was full of paintings done by his wife, pictures of her and the two of them together as he reminisced about events in their lives. She was a beautiful, creative powerful presence, whose absence he was struggling to come to terms with. He was, as the advocates reported, anxious, depressed, silently angry and resigned. Mr F was not only struggling with his diagnosis and the onset of dementia, he was also in deep bereavement.

During the twelve-month counselling treatment we offered, Mr F was given the opportunity to talk about his wife's death, their relationship and was enabled to mourn. Similarly, he was helped to think about his diagnosis and the losses he was experiencing. He reconnected with family and friends and joined services which enriched his daily life.

Fleur Sharman, head of the Dementia Advocacy Service reviewed him after the end of our sessions and commented:

> Mr F was seen for a review of his care package a year later. Upon meeting with him, I saw a marked improvement in his overall demeanour, wellbeing and in particular in his level of engagement. He presented without anxiety, was calm and was interested in discussions regarding his care support and the future. Between our initial contact in 2007 and our next interactions with him in 2008 the only significant change had been the counselling support he had engaged with. His medication had remained unchanged and he had accessed no further social support such as day care services or befriending. It was clear that during 2008 he developed confidence and autonomy, his communication had improved, he was calm and his relationships with his next-of-kin had improved significantly.

Observations on the impact of therapeutic contact

We found that a year of counselling did have a positive impact. In many cases we observed one or more of the following:

- Increased capacity to relate to people
- Better communication and cognitive functioning

- Improvement in mood
- Increased empowerment
- Improved relationships with others

Responses and feedback from some of the users of the service, their carers and relatives were very encouraging and our sense was that our clients were benefiting from this work. Many responded in a way which showed that they had internalised a valuable experience and clearly used the sessions for support. One significant problem, as can be seen in these examples, is that of ending. Unfortunately the constraints of funding did not allow for work to continue in an open-ended manner. In some cases, such as Mrs A, the client found a way of managing the ending. She seemed to have internalised a good experience which she would carry with her and she had valued the support she received at a time of great change.

The ending in the case of Mrs G was difficult as Mrs G displayed a cognitive and emotional recovery by the end of a year of therapy as well as a strong attachment to her counsellor – probably the first of its kind in her life. In this time she had been enabled to connect with a family friend and with other services which provided social contact and activities. The ending had to be managed very carefully and had been brought into the work half way through the treatment. It was nevertheless extremely painful for both therapist and client.

In the case of Mr F the work had resulted in very clear improvement as well. He was given the opportunity to work through his profound loss, he recovered his verbal and a significant part of his cognitive functions, he was able to advocate for himself with services and with family and his relations with friends and family improved.

Further developments

The Talking Therapies Project was mainstreamed in 2008 and so was embedded in the general Counselling Service of Age UK Camden. Ten percent of clients seen by the service suffer from dementia. Due to funding cuts, clients can only receive twenty sessions. Integration into the main Counselling Service represents Age UK Camden's core belief that people with memory problems should be integrated into the wider community, a policy they implement in their community centres and across the services they offer. For this reason a member of the Memory Clinic is also employed permanently by the organisation. Furthermore, a vital initiative is being implemented in collaboration with the organisation Relationships which addresses the impact of the illness on the couple. Couples are helped to process the diagnosis and make the adjustments they need to make as they face a different and difficult set of circumstances. Volunteer counsellors on the service receive training to work with affected couples (Balfour, 2015).

In conclusion

Working with clients with dementia evokes in therapists much that is terrifying and painful. In the same way that the client is vulnerable, so do we have to be vulnerable in order to work at relational depth. Like our clients, we too must be genuine. Moreover, it can be seen from the cases described that because of the acuteness of need, the counsellor is required to extend herself beyond the therapeutic role on an emotional, mental and practical level. Danuta Lipinska sums the complexity of this role poignantly:

> I believe that as a counsellor, I am called to stand in the gap for the clients: the gap between who they were and who they are becoming; the gap between their home and the care environment; the gap between family and professionals; the gap between members of the family; the gap between life and death, joy and misery; the gap between heaven and earth. I want to continue to value and encourage that person's right to be here still and the right to make an impression.
>
> (Lipinska, 2009, p. 74)

Acknowledgements

I would like to thank all the staff at Age UK Camden for their support in the development of the Talking Therapies Project and in particular David Richards, Monica Riveros and Gary Jones as well as all the volunteers who carried out the work and provided the material included in this paper.

References

Alzheimer's Society (2016). *Facts for the Media.* Available at: www.alzheimers.org.uk/info/20027/news_and_media/ . . . /facts_for_the_media. Accessed 16 June 2016.

Balfour, A. (2015). *Living Together with Dementia: A Relationship Intervention for Couples Living with Dementia.* https://tavistockrelationships.org/images/TCCR_summary_of_the_LTwD_approach_Nov_2015_-_FINAL.pdf Accessed 21 October 2017.

Kitwood, T. (1990). Psychotherapy and Dementia. *British Psychological Society, Psychotherapy Section Newsletter, 8* (June): 40–56.

Kitwood, T. (1997). *Dementia Reconsidered: The Person Comes First.* Buckingham: Open University Press.

Lipinska, D. (2009). *Person-Centred Counselling for People with Dementia.* London: Jessica Kingsley.

Richards, D. (2011). Working with older LGBT people. *Therapy Today, 22 (10):* 11–14.

Waddell, M. (2007). Only links between early and later life. In: R. Davenhill (Ed.), *Looking Into Later Life: A Psychoanalytic Approach to Depression and Dementia in Old Age,* pp. 187–200. London: Karnac.

Windle, K., Wagland, R., Forder, J., D'Amico, F., Janssen, D., & Wistow, G. (2009). The National Evaluation of Partnerships for Older People Projects: Executive Summary. Available at www.pssru.ac.uk/pdf/rs053.pdf. Accessed 24 July 2013.

Chapter 11

Reflections on the conference
Exploring Attachment, Memory
Loss and Ageing
20th Sept 2014

Valerie Sinason

I interviewed John Bowlby shortly after I began the child psychotherapy training at the Tavistock Clinic. Indeed, like many people, the two names were, for me, synonymous with each other. Indeed, it was thanks to Dr Bowlby and Mrs. Martha Harris (Mattie) that the child psychotherapy training was established. However, following his official retirement, John Bowlby paid for his own room and loyal secretarial support – the development of his research ideas on attachment had travelled round the world more speedily than in his own home – as so often happens!

I joined The Bowlby Centre for a number of reasons primarily because of the impact of Bowlby's work on my understanding, and in order to have a home for my attachment-based adult work as well as my continuing pleasure in its journal and conferences. Indeed, the Centre, with attachment seen as the lens through which all human relating happens, is internationally known for the way it tackles some of the most painful issues of our time in its sought-after conferences.

Attachment, memory, loss, dementia and ageing are not popular psychoanalytic subjects. Coming close to death as the ultimate taboo subject, with our ubiquitous struggle to face our own mortality, this conference also covered the death of the mind.

It has often been the oldest and most distinguished members of our different societies who get burdened with the task of talking about this subject, as if, being older, they will have a better grasp of it! Indeed, it was at a conference on ageing that I first had the pleasure of meeting the psychoanalyst Pearl King who chaired the day and was to be my supervisor for the next few decades. It was thanks to Pearl (who lived until the age of 95) that the Institute of Psychoanalysis allowed trainees over the age of 40 to be accepted into the analytic training, an age Freud, full of self-doubt about himself at 40, considered too old to change.

This conference offered artistic creativity, research, theory, personal experiences and pioneering projects and there were both highly alert eyes in the conference room as I sat chairing the morning and wet eyes.

Pam Schweitzer, MBE, founded Age Exchange Theatre Trust in 1983 through brilliantly understanding the need for Reminiscence Theatre and indeed she opened the first Reminiscence Centre in London in 1987. Anastasia Patrikiou brought in therapeutic approaches and Sir Richard Bowlby vividly showed how early trauma impacted on later memory. Hazel Leventhal brought her own care for her older sister into her moving relational talk, Kate White brought the personal and professional into her powerful presentation on the attachment perspective and Angela Cotter brought in her nursing home manager experience that came from a deep personal understanding of the field.

All were part of a profound mosaic made with the highly moved and involved audience. We will all be biased as to which extract from such a day stays with us most and very personal reasons why.

For me, the short film *Ex Memoria* by Josh Appignanesi was an unforgettable jewel in the crown in the way it was both a perfect piece in its own right but cast light on all presentations both before and after it was screened.

Lasting only sixteen minutes, Josh uses his grandmother's own painful experiences of living in a nursing home, to inform his moving film. Eva, a character in her 70s played with extraordinary sensibility by Sara Kestelman, is a Polish Jewish refugee and the film is shot from her point of view. In addition to the painful issues that came from his grandmother's life that went into her character he collaborated with the Bradford Dementia Group and gained funding from the Wellcome Trust's Sciart scheme. (The trust coined the term "sciart" in 1996, giving its backing for interdisciplinary research into science, humanities and the arts.)

Eva relives fragments of her adolescent trauma in Nazi-invaded Poland. She sees the rooms and corridors and stairs of the care home as part of the scenery of that trauma, and thanks to the brilliant filming, so do we. Without the need for words we visually share in her perception, the missing jigsaw pieces, pockets of trauma, hope and clarity. Very rarely in such a film we see her offering herself sexually to care staff to save her life. In my work in old people's homes I have found it so painful to witness the way sexuality is dealt with due to unresolved issues of the carers. What I will never forget is the kindly care assistant who does not reject this behaviour but understands where it comes from and this allows her to come back into the present. For a moment. And with just one carer.

Tackling traumatic sexual display in the elderly is a double taboo and to see it tackled this beautifully and lovingly brought tears of recognition. It could only have been created by a loving family member.

It is not surprising to find that since this miniature masterpiece, Josh Appignanesi has produced *New Man* with his partner about the couple's pregnancy and birth of twins. This has been a full length mainstream cinema film with excellent critical reviews.

Here is a poem *Alzheimer's Disease* which I wrote when a patient I worked with, a brilliant academic, died of Alzheimer's. I have written about him in my book *Mental Handicap and the Human Condition* (Sinason, 2010). I visited him every week to provide on-site therapy as he would have got lost coming to see me. It was at the point where he had flashcards on the furniture spelling out "bed", "table" etc and then could not even read those words, that in tears, I went to supervision with Anne Alvarez and wrote this poem to process and mourn.

Alzheimer's Disease

He sits holding his head
On the stiff armchair
In the spare bedroom
The old help sleeps
Together they have watched the house
Empty itself

The children left the house
Like a flock of birds
The leaves left the trees
Even the cars left the street
Leaving the houses like thin stalks

And his brain is leaving him
Each day it erases itself
His sentences end in a silver trail
A daily funeral

Yesterday all place names left him forever
Today it was numbers
The shadow of an atlas crosses his face

Today the old help forgot to make
Him lunch
Today he forgot he had not eaten

Touching the family photographs
Like a fading Braille
He sits with his head in his hands on the stiff armchair.

Valerie Sinason (*Night Shift*, 1995, p. 25)

And here was a poem that came from my work in an old people's home.

Over and Out

Sun through the tall windows
And the dayroom is empty
Filipino assistants are disinfecting the floors
Scrubbing at shadows of loss and incontinence
While the owners of the shadows

are wheeled into the garden to dry
Round bright tables and under the parasols
Loudspeakers are blaring an end-of-pier song
No-one knows that no-one is talking
The nurses have lost their native land and tongue
The residents have lost.

Myra the volunteer bursts in like a speedboat
Leaving ripples of movement wherever she goes
She goes fast for fear of falling over and out
Into the waters of loss

On and on she rushes
Drawing out and catching the precious fish of memory
Only to throw it back into the rising waters
She leaves with her own name
Resounding in her ears
Uttered by half the accents of Europe
She goes before she drowns in it
The sun goes on and on

Valerie Sinason (*Night Shift*, 1995, p. 13)

A last poem concerns my maternal grandfather who I only met in the last decade of his life, forty years after he had left his first wife, my grandmother, and his three children. As he lay dying his second wife, with whom he had had a happy marriage, was suffering with dementia in a care home.

It has come to this

It has come to this
The old man is dying in the geriatric ward
His sharp mind watches his heart stumble
His old wife is in a nursing home
Five miles away
Her heart beats strong
While her mind dements

There are no personal phones to link them
Only tired hostile nurses

The old woman has forgotten
Her husband is in hospital
She thinks he came last week

And stole her biscuit tin
She thinks he came the day before
And stole her grapes
The nurses have given up reminding her
She erases as fast as they speak
She is rubbing their good years
Out of her memory
Faster than his heart slows

The estranged children return to the fold
First to the hospital bed
Then to the nursing home
The house crumbles between them
Whatever is touched leaves an ugly mark
All struggle to stay clear.

Valerie Sinason, unpublished poem

It is seminal conferences like this which help to bring greater clarity to a reality that impacts on us so deeply.

References

Appignanesi, J. (2006). *Ex Memoria.* A film directed by Josh Appignanesi. Missing in Action Films, London.

Appignanesi, J., & Baum, D. (2016). *The New Man.* A documentary film directed by Josh Appignanesi & Devorah Baum. Mercenary Films, London.

Sinason, V. (1995). *Night Shift.* London: Karnac.

Sinason, V. (2010). *Mental Handicap and the Human Condition: An Analytic Approach to Intellectual Disability.* London: Free Association Books.

Index